What people are saying about

Let's Talk About Doubt

I am so grateful that Kat Wordsworth is inviting peo[...] about doubt by going public with her story. While the writings of theologians and pastors on doubt can be helpful, there is something especially helpful about a "lay person" who is honest without being cynical and hopeful without being unrealistic. Kat Wordsworth's book could be your guide in discovering for yourself how to be a doubtful Christian.
Brian D. McLaren, author of *Do I Stay Christian?* and *Faith After Doubt*

This book is a gift, Kat writes beautifully about her journey with doubt, her writing is infused with hope and her words will be a balm to fellow questioning souls.
Rachael Newham, author of *And Yet* and Mental Health Friendly Church Project Manager at Kintsugi Hope

From the very first pages, Wordsworth puts into words thoughts and feelings that many will have barely dared articulate to themselves. Her writing is tender and unflinching, compassionate and honest. This book is for anyone who feels on the fringes of the church and fears they are alone in their wondering, wrestling and wavering.
Florence Gildea, author of *Lessons I Have Unlearned*

In recent years, the Western church has sought to paper over the cracks of people's questions and wonderings in favor of presenting a happier, slicker, easier Christianity. *Let's Talk About Doubt* is the book we've all been waiting for, whether or not we've acknowledged it. With gentleness, grace and good humor, Kat Wordsworth presents an articulate picture of doubt and what it feels like. Her words are neither glibly victorious nor pessimistically depressing, but full of hope that doubt can exist within the realms of faith in our sovereign creator God. If you are a doubter, you will find solace within the pages of this book. If you are not, you will find enlightenment — which is why I not only heartily recommend it, but strongly *urge* every Christian to read it.

Lucy Rycroft, founder of thehopefilledfamily.com and author of *Redeeming Advent* and *Deborah and Jael*

Let's Talk About Doubt

A story of doubt, faith
and life in between

Let's Talk About Doubt

A story of doubt, faith
and life in between

Kat Wordsworth

CIRCLE
BOOKS

Winchester, UK
Washington, USA

JOHN HUNT PUBLISHING

First published by Circle Books, 2023
Circle Books is an imprint of John Hunt Publishing Ltd., No. 3 East St., Alresford,
Hampshire SO24 9EE, UK
office@jhpbooks.com
www.johnhuntpublishing.com
www.circle-books.com

For distributor details and how to order please visit the 'Ordering' section on our website.

Text copyright: Kat Wordsworth 2021

ISBN: 978 1 80341 156 9
978 1 80341 157 6 (ebook)
Library of Congress Control Number: 2021953213

Scripture quotations taken from The Holy Bible, New International Version (Anglicised edition)
Copyright 1979, 1984, 2011 by Biblica (formerly International Bible Society). Used by permission of Hodder & Stoughton Publishers, an Hachette UK company. All rights reserved. 'NIV' is a
registered trademark of Biblica (formerly International Bible Society). UK trademark number
1448790.

Design: Stuart Davies

UK: Printed and bound by CPI Group (UK) Ltd, Croydon, CR0 4YY
US: Printed and bound by Thomson Shore, 7300 West Joy Road, Dexter, MI 48130

Contents

For my family, both related and not.

Acknowledgments

To everyone who has patiently listened to my questions, anger and tears, thank you. To everyone who has stood by me, whether they share my doubts or not, thank you. To everyone that has supported and encouraged me in my little corner of the internet, I can't tell you how much of a difference it has made.

To Noah and Annie, thank you for giving me a reason to try and make a difference. And to Paddy, thank you for your love and for always knowing when I need a cup of tea.

Prologue

Breaking the Cycle

Let's talk about doubt. Not a phrase that I have ever heard in church, whether spoken from the pulpit or whispered in the pews. Whatever the reason for this silence; maybe fear, misunderstanding or simply the fact that we aren't very good at talking about difficult things, the end result is the same. Doubt is not often a visible conversation. Talking about it is the exception not the rule. But make no mistake. Just because doubt is not spoken about openly doesn't mean that it isn't there. Scratch the surface and questions are being asked. We live within the tension that although doubt is normal, it is not normalized. Although it is common, it is not often communal. The reality of doubt is kept private, the conversations hidden behind closed doors.

The absence of doubt within the public spaces of Christian culture has several consequences. First and foremost: experiencing doubt can become desperately tangled with feelings of isolation, shame and fear. If you have never heard it discussed and can't see anywhere obvious to turn to for help then you can be left feeling adrift and alone. Hidden in the pews, suffering in silence. The impression that doubt isn't discussed because questions are unacceptable or because you are the only one to have them is difficult to escape from. Within this atmosphere of secrecy and silence, the threat of rejection and the loss of community become very real fears. Doubts can spiral out of control.

Secondly: the ability of friends and family to offer meaningful support can be severely damaged. Unless people have personal or vicarious experience, conversations about doubt (even when people have the best intentions) can become messy and inflict further pain. Not speaking openly about doubt in a corporate context threatens to leave us with a communal gap in wisdom.

This book is my attempt to break the cycle of shame and isolation. As an intensely private and reserved person, I am an unlikely candidate to attempt such a feat. But weathering the storm of doubt in my own life has unleashed within me the stubborn resolve to try. To do all that I can to prevent what happened to me happening to anyone else.

For those of you whose stories have played out in the midst of this dissonance, the purpose of sharing my story is to offer you company and comfort. If you take nothing else from what I have written, please know this: you are not alone, you are not a failure and your wrestling is sacred. There is nothing weak about experiencing doubt. Nothing weak about wrestling with such overwhelming questions, nothing weak about finding the courage to be honest with yourself and others. I appreciate that I am talking about my personal experience of doubt and that not everyone will recognize or relate to the specifics of my experience. But I hope that even if the details vary, it will still help to diminish isolation. We don't have to follow exactly the same path in order to offer each other sanctuary.

For those of you who want to support friends or family, or simply want to learn more about the impact of doubt, I hope that sharing my experience will lower the risk of misunderstanding and help equip you to make conversations about doubt as helpful as possible.

Let me be clear from the start. I am not offering a treatise on doubt or a step-by-step guide to overcoming it. Neither is this book a confrontational attack on any particular individual, church or denomination. All that I am offering is my honesty. My story, with nothing polished or glossed over and nothing omitted to spare me any embarrassment. I'm well aware that it might be as uncomfortable to read as it was to write. Not only does doubt carry a stigma, but we are a culture that dislikes lingering in the middle of our stories. We crave resolution, the light at the end of the tunnel and the perfect cadence. Our instinct is to fix, heal and move on from A to B as swiftly as possible. It's no wonder that life in the unresolved space of doubt can be so difficult to bear. It goes against everything we were taught to expect from life. So even if my story makes you shift in your seat, I hope you can see that dwelling on the mess and speaking from the heart of doubt is necessary. For if stories are only ever shared in hindsight, with the rough edges and darkest moments smoothed over, people in the midst of their pain will feel a total lack of connection. In the context of doubt, these tales of happily ever after can make you feel further isolated and alone.

Two disclaimers before we begin. One: I acknowledge that my story and understanding has been formed within the confines of my background, culture and personal experience. If your experience of church and Christian culture is one where doubt is welcomed and openly discussed, please know that I intend no offence. That's not what this book is. And two: I don't wear doubt as a badge of honor. I don't think that it makes me a better, cleverer or deeper person than anyone else. I don't believe that faith cannot be real unless you have wrestled through doubt. It appears that many people go through a time of sorting out or asking questions, but I don't believe that to be necessary for faith, or that doubt is always the catalyst for that season if it does occur. The point of this book isn't to drive any kind of wedge between those who doubt and those who don't. It's not us versus them, it's about creating understanding and connection on both sides.

This is my story. It is a story of messy, difficult, doubtful faith. The door is wedged open. The conversation no longer hidden. Painful and uncomfortable at times, but a necessary antidote. Let's talk about doubt.

Part I

Lost

On the outside looking in

My earliest memory of church is sitting on the floor in between pews, playing with a notebook, pencils and miniature stories of the parables. I can remember the smell of the leather handbag that my mum kept them in, as well as the brown glass coffee cups and crispy, unyielding toilet paper that were seemingly universal features of English churches in the 1990s.

With perfect attendance from the womb onwards, my life ticked every Christian box possible. I was raised in a Christian home, I went to youth groups and youth church, then onto a university Christian Union alongside another church. I knew the Bible well, I read Christian books, I went to Christian festivals and I listened to worship music. I did everything that I thought was expected of me. But underneath the seemingly perfect exterior, doubts had been present for a long time, even if I hadn't given them that name. I had always been aware of a nagging sense that something was missing, as though I was waiting for something to click into place. What I felt didn't match up with what I heard people describe, or what was declared from the front of church. The elusive personal relationship. Assurance, joy and companionship. For many years, I kept these feelings dampened with the assumption that at some point, something would happen to take me to the next level.

My early faith was built on a dubious footing: an unhealthy combination of waiting for something more to happen and relying on other people. I desperately clung to the coat tails of others, captivated by people whose faith almost visibly radiated out from them, with the hope that it might rub off on me. My faith was not my own.

It was with this already crumbling foundation that I began work as a worship intern at a church after university. Why I applied is an interesting question. Hindsight has been a tricky lens to manage when looking back at my faith prior to its collapse. I suspect that my mind has dismissed now what I genuinely thought was faith then. I don't believe that I explicitly lied to secure the position, although there is no doubt that having grown up in church, by the age of 21 I was skilled in the art of knowing the right things to say. Perhaps I was subconsciously hoping that the belong, behave, believe adage would come true for me, and quickly.

About a month in to my internship, I went to a worship leaders conference. The festering questions, insecurities and doubts converged. The intensity of the conference made it impossible for me to carry on ignoring that I was the odd one out. I finally caught sight of the mask that I had worn for years and the effort to maintain the façade became too much to bear. People's certainty, passion, faith: I couldn't hide from the fact that I didn't feel the same way. The click that I had been waiting for hadn't come and I lost hope that it would. Ignoring my doubts for so long had not made them go away. Instead, the questions had turned septic, an infected open wound, spreading deep into my heart and mind.

I locked myself into a toilet cubicle during a break and the truth of my situation swept over me in waves. There was a lot that was still unknown to me, deeper reasons for why my faith was vulnerable which I will discuss over the course of this book. All I knew in that moment was that I was different. I didn't belong and I didn't understand. It wasn't the specifics of the conference that mattered, and neither was it the fault of my job. With such unstable foundations, it was an accident waiting to happen.

Like a knot that appears secure until you tug at it and the whole thing collapses, in that cubicle I had a complete unraveling of faith.

Perhaps this is a fatal flaw in my reasoning, but it wasn't that I decided that everyone else was making it up. The message that sank deeply into me was that there was something wrong with me, something that meant I was incapable of believing it was real. I'd had my chance, had all the same opportunities as those around me, done all the same things, but still found myself sitting in a different room. Or to be accurate, hiding in the toilet.

I was on the outside, looking in.

Eventually I left the cubicle. Returned to normality feeling everything except normal. Questions whirled, with one surfacing more than others. Had I ever been a Christian in the first place? Had I lost my faith or realized that it had never actually been there? Despite the years that have passed, it is still a question that I don't know the answer to. If you look for guidance on how to persevere through a season of doubt, the advice is almost always to focus on past times, past anchor points of faith. Don't dwell on the darkness and use the memories to pull you through. Most of the Christians I know seem to have had at least one defining light bulb moment where they knew for sure that it was all true. Where they experienced something undeniable. In seasons of difficulty or darkness, the memory of these anchor points serves as a source of strength and hope. The problem was that I didn't have that. People kept telling me to remember God's past goodness to me, moments of encounter, of healing, of answered prayer, but I couldn't think of any. I didn't have my own story, anything to fall back on.

My earliest memories of church jump from playing in the

pews to a much later event, when I overheard a post-church conversation between my mum and a close friend, discussing how hard it was to be a Christian. I'm not sure what the context was, but my young mind twisted it into meaning that there was some sort of grueling, gladiator style initiation test that you had to undergo to become a Christian. Years later, I know that the reality is a much more challenging test of endurance than the assault course that I imagined.

Category four storm

One of the first hurdles you face with doubt is language. Definition and interpretation. Doubt is an umbrella term which can mean a variety of different things to different people. Very broadly speaking, I think doubts within a Christian context fall into one of four groups. Doubts about theology, either particular doctrines or biblical interpretation, doubts about God's personality and nature, doubts stemming from the way other denominations or other Christians behave, and at the deepest level, doubts about God's existence. But even within those sweeping headlines, there are other things which people often lump in with doubt, including disappointment, anger, unanswered prayer, disillusionment and grievances with particular church leaders. The word has also become interchangeable with questioning, something which I think carries a different undertone.

The cumulative effect of these overlapping definitions is that the meaning of doubt gets muddy; an automatic barrier to effective communication.

When I tried to talk to people shortly after the cubicle moment, most assumed that my doubt fell into one of the first three categories. That I had a problem with a particular aspect of Christianity; perhaps hell, suffering or other religions.

Not that I didn't find those things almost insurmountable at times, but they weren't the tipping point. Maybe people would have found that easier to deal with. I definitely would have. Individual topics became distractions in themselves over the years. Perhaps if I can just resolve this, then things will fall into place. Well, maybe this then. Or this.

Whether correct or not, the assumption that I made in these conversations was that there is a hierarchy of which doubts are considered most palatable. Most acceptable, most fixable are the first three; questions of theology, apologetics and community. Stalling at the bottom sits the most unwelcome and unacceptable doubt: the question of God's existence.

So let me be crystal clear, cards on the table. When I say that I doubt, I don't mean that I began to question an aspect of God's character, or that I was struggling with a specific doctrine or tradition of church. What I mean is that I struggle to believe that God actually exists. It is a category four storm. Blunt, but necessary to say. I'm often too scared to admit it in such a forceful, conversation stopping way. Being a people pleaser and a doubter is a hard tightrope to balance.

It was at this point that shame, fear and isolation entered my story. It is this part of my experience that motivates me to talk about doubt. For I can't help but wonder how differently the next few years of my life would have turned out if, having recognized and admitted my doubts, I'd had the courage to be totally honest, to myself and others. If I'd known that doubt wasn't a dirty secret that I needed to keep to myself. There were people trying to support me, both colleagues and friends, but I assumed that admitting how deep my doubt went would horrify them. I allowed shame to lie. And it definitely was a lie, because years later, when I finally found the strength to be honest, those same friends and colleagues didn't flinch.

Too ashamed to admit the substance of my doubts, I fell silent. I turned in on myself, with the thought that there was something fundamentally wrong with me rapidly gaining potency and power. The infection spread.

October 2009

How long, LORD? Will you forget me for ever?
How long will you hide your face from me?
How long must I wrestle with my thoughts
and day after day have sorrow in my heart? Psalm 13.1–2

What strength do I have, that I should still hope?
What prospects, that I should be patient?
Do I have the strength of stone?
Is my flesh bronze? Job 6.11–12

I am stagnant. Stuck in no man's land. I don't even know what the problem is anymore. The whole thing feels like an impenetrable cloud. I don't know where or how to begin so I have retreated into the safety of numbness. I become more hardened as each day passes. How do I get out of here?

Darkness is my closest friend

Looking back, I think the most surprising thing about my story is that it doesn't end here. I suspect that it has for countless others. Finding myself in such an emotionally unbearable situation, with the world as I knew it dissolving beneath my feet, why didn't I save myself the agony and walk away?

The simple answer is that I couldn't. I was completely trapped by my circumstances. I had no friends or family that weren't Christians. My financial security was dependent on working at church. I didn't have anywhere else to go. The longer answer is what comprises the rest of this book.

The immediate impact of the moment in the toilet cubicle was that I felt like an outsider in every situation. My job, my home, my social life; it felt as though I didn't belong anywhere. The effort of pretending that nothing had changed and the perceived threat of being found out was exhausting. Instead of opening up and admitting what had happened, my instinct was to carry on as if nothing had changed. Wear a mask, pretend, hide. It wasn't a malicious or manipulative decision, it was fear, pure and simple. But adding that constant tension to my already broken heart and relentless questioning made mental health problems seemingly inescapable for me. Suppression of my questions, masked by distraction, became my way of life.

It seems obvious in hindsight, but the truth is that if you try to live a life where you can't even face your own thoughts, it breaks you.

And so, the darkness crept in. Weaved its way into my thought processes, gnawed its way into my confidence and my very personality. The fear took hold and life felt out of control.

Anxiety is often described as an irrational worry or rational worry taken out of proportion. But for a Christian who loses their faith, how can anxiety ever be irrational or out of proportion? The world is a terrifying place to be if you have no hope that there is more to life than it appears. It felt to me as though most people were either purposefully deluding themselves about the reality of life or else able to numb themselves to it in a way that I couldn't manage. My brain simply wouldn't let me forget. Anxiety forced me then, and still does sometimes now, to live with the worst case scenario tainting every second with fear. And it wasn't just the present moment. Every thought of the future, every memory of the past was marred, spoilt by an unrelenting barrage of what ifs. I found it difficult to remember that I hadn't always felt that way. I looked back to times before the anxiety took hold and couldn't believe that I lived without fear as my constant companion.

The anxiety was obvious; I couldn't not notice the change in my behavior, the way I felt when I left the house. But the depression was much subtler. It took a long time to recognize and accept that at some point, I crossed the line between feeling miserable some of the time to feeling completely engulfed by depression.

Spoiler alert: there are other things going on in my body that made identifying the depression tricky, and it's still not clear to me where one thing starts and other things end. But what is clear is that at some point, the weight of all the pain and emotional turmoil settled. Took up heavy residence in my heart and mind and spread its tendrils throughout my body.

The relationship between anxiety and depression can sometimes seem contradictory. One slows you down, one speeds you up. My experience of living with the two side by side was a bit like being on an unpredictable seesaw. If one condition was particularly bad, particularly weighty, the other seemed to get subdued, lighter. What is clear is that the combination of both made for an extremely unsettled, miserable and agitated existence. And definitely not an ideal place to deal with crippling doubts. In the words of Psalm 88.18, at times it felt like darkness was my closest friend.

* * *

It's important to note that although I can connect the dots between my doubt and my mental health in hindsight, the cause of these problems wasn't clear to me at the time. My brain ran out of capacity to think outside of itself. I focused simply on getting through each day. It's also important to point out that although it has helped, making the connections didn't lead to an automatic escape route. Sadly, life just isn't that straightforward.

Even now, years later, it's hard to admit this stuff. It feels embarrassing to put these words out into the world. But I choose to share it for two reasons. One: although things have improved, mental health problems still carry a stigma. People find it incredibly hard to open up about their struggles. Combine that with the stigma of doubt and you end up in a very uncomfortable position, at high risk of isolation and misunderstanding. Which leads me to reason number two: awareness. Doubt cuts deep. Mental health problems aren't the impact of doubt for everyone, but they are for some. It can have a wide ranging effect on our hearts and minds. And unless people start talking about that, the stigma will remain, the support offered will not be sufficient and the isolation will continue.

June 2010

Suppose one of you has a hundred sheep and loses one of them. Doesn't he leave the ninety-nine in the open country and go after the lost sheep until he finds it? And when he finds it, he joyfully puts it on his shoulders and goes home. Luke 15.4–6

The infamous lost sheep: wandered off, got lost, had to be rescued. Did it forget how to get back? Did it get distracted by some fresh grass? Perhaps it got stuck in some thorns. Unable to return to the shepherd, totally dependent on being rescued, but still fighting to get free. Becoming further tangled, ensnared and injured. The parallel with my situation feels clear. I am lost. But as for the other side of the story? Is God really searching for me? It feels so one-sided, that I have searched for years but got nothing in return, twisting and turning in the thorns, doing serious damage to my head and my heart. Is it supposed to be like this? Am I doing something wrong or have I wandered too far, past the point of return?

I'm not sure how long I can carry on. I think about it all constantly. Going to church is emotional torture. I feel like a dud, an awkward add on, an eavesdropper. What am I doing to myself? At what point will self-preservation kick in to stop me destroying myself with this heartbreak?

Mind the gap

From the first book to the last, the Bible presents us with the stories of an unlikely cast of characters. Shepherds, kings, judges, fishermen, tentmakers: their stories join to offer hope and wisdom and demonstrate God's habits of redemption, forgiveness and grace. But adjust the lens slightly and the same stories can be seen as something else. Stories of people who wrestled with God, questioning his goodness, his intentions, his plans, his power, his resurrection and his presence. The Bible is full of people who doubted God. So strong is the silence about doubt within the church that I feel as though that last sentence should be whispered.

One of the places where this tension is at its most obvious is in the Psalms, which might explain why a common response when you tell a Christian that you are struggling with your faith is an encouragement to read through this book. And at times, I do just that. It makes sense, the outpouring of emotion and brutal honesty directed at God can be hugely comforting. I read Psalms of lament, Psalms that dwell on a desperate, life threatening need for God. Psalms that express anger, questioning, rejection and longing. Of course they offer some comfort. I feel a connection, I feel understood. Often they are the only things that I can bear to read in the Bible.

My God, my God, why have you forsaken me?
Why are you so far from saving me,
so far from my cries of anguish?
My God, I cry out by day, but you do not answer,
by night, but I find no rest. Psalm 22.1–2

But you don't get far without noticing that the normal pattern, even when the Psalmist begins in abject despair, is for the Psalm to end in praise. With hope, faith and confidence. Remembering past times of love, rescue and joy. Take a look at the end of Psalm 22, which ends with triumph and praise, even after starting in such misery. The notable exception is Psalm 88. Thank goodness for Psalm 88. The general rule is that lament, pain and suffering are woven alongside praise. And this is exactly why people suggest reading them. They hope that seeing the example will stop you from remaining in the darkness and prompt you to move on. We are a people who crave the ability to fix problems as quickly as possible. Gratitude and thanksgiving, offered despite pain, is recognized as being helpful to those who are struggling. But on the darkest days of doubt, when you don't feel able to follow the model presented in the Psalms without it being a complete lie, reading them is a jolt that can leave you feeling cold and hopeless.

How did they get out of the depths to end up praising God? What happened to turn things around? Why has God answered, rescued and delivered them but not me?

Psalms read as a completed account, and it took me a while to realize that I had to be mindful of the gaps. Gaps in time between the experiences and the writing, gaps in time to reflect and learn. I've started highlighting the blank space between the stanzas where the mood shifts. It stops me from moving from one verse to another without pausing to remember that time might have elapsed. It also allows me a slither of hope that one day I might look back on this time with the hindsight of another gap, one that has allowed me to move forward a few verses.

* * *

Awareness of gaps between the experience and the retelling is important for my story too. Time has elapsed between the toilet moment and now. Well over a decade. It has not been years of calm acceptance, diligent and earnest searching, or even the desire to try. In all honesty, I have spent most of the time with my head stuck firmly in the sand. With bitterness, anger and pain building, fueled by the lack of progress and repeated damaging experiences. I have no intention of sugar coating this story to paint myself in a better light. It would be a betrayal not only of myself, but of those who need to know that someone has walked the same road that they now find themselves on. The point I want to firmly impress is that it has taken me years to confront and form my thoughts into what you read here; years to even allow my brain space to begin to process them. I don't tell it in order to incite guilt or shame if you are a step or two behind. Don't judge your own story by pressing fast forward on mine.

January 2012

The distractions were intentional. Burying my head in the sand taken to a new level. A way to anesthetize myself to the pain. Self-protection, barriers raised, refusing myself permission to feel. And the options were forthcoming and seemingly endless. Voracious reading, countless must see TV series and films, apps to soothe me to sleep, a never ending list of jobs, a whole world of entertainment a click away in my pocket. Western culture doesn't seem to encourage contemplation. Embrace it, and you will never have a moment unoccupied. So I did.

But at some point, the tool became a habit. I was too enthusiastic in my application and it went too far. Distraction grew from being an isolated coping strategy into my whole way of life. It exerted its influence over my physical and mental processes, my whole rhythm of being. My mind is disjointed, frantic, flitting from one thing to another without space to consider anything. My attention isn't just dulled to the pain, but to everything in life. To my relationships, my work and myself.

There is no doubt in my mind that this way of living has contributed to and exacerbated my physical and mental health problems. My ability to relax and rest, during which time you heal and recover, is almost non-existent. Rest brings with it inevitable quiet. Space. Time. A chance for thoughts to develop.

All things that I have fought so hard to avoid.

I have been smothered by the comfort blanket of distraction.

If you presented me with this lifestyle, showed me the reality, my fragmented thought processes, my body in tatters, never any substance to my thoughts, there is no way that I would accept it. It didn't even help long term with the problems. You can't force yourself to forget this kind of thing and the pain has just seeped out in other ways. But in a cruel twist, I can't seem to break free from the spell.

I have tried. I switched my phone off for a day a week, set limits on my obsessive checking of the news, slowed down my speed reading, challenged myself to embrace the silence. The benefits were immediate and obvious: my mind was calmer, I felt more in tune with myself and significantly less disjointed. But I slipped. I was drawn back to the familiar, the safety of the cotton wool option.

Something needs to shift. Progress seems unlikely if I don't allow any space or silence for God to actually answer me. The habits and addictions need to be broken. But I'm scared. I introduced the distraction on purpose. What will be left if the white noise has gone? Will I be forced to confront the unrelenting absence of God? Or will there be a voice waiting to fill the void?

Dominoes

The damage that doubt inflicted didn't stop with my mental health. A chain of dominoes was set in motion that day in the toilet cubicle, an unstoppable toppling which paid no attention to the barrier that we often pretend exists between mental and physical health. I couldn't contain the impact and the ripple effects quickly spilled out from a purely cerebral, intellectual box into my self-image, sense of identity and physical health.

Trauma is a difficult word. Using it makes me feel like a fraud; how dare I apply such a strong word to my story when others experience such horrific things. And of course, there is no comparison. But over the years that followed my crisis, it became difficult to deny that I had been traumatized. For me, the root of the trauma circled around the idea of safety. Ignoring my questions and plowing on with life regardless meant that I was repeatedly putting myself into situations and conversations where my body perceived a threat. The threat of rejection, the threat of being found out, the threat of hell. Church, a place which I had always known as a place of connection and community became a place where I felt deeply unsafe. In these situations, my body tried to protect me by placing me on high alert. I was flooded with adrenaline, ready to fight or run. Ready to escape or defend myself. But I did neither. I sat, for years, swallowing my questions, allowing my body no outlet for the tension which raced through it.

The question of safety for me was mostly relational and psychological. And it was almost exclusively perceived rather than real. I am painfully aware that for some people the issue of safety in church goes much further. Physical safety can be at risk. The threat is real. My trauma is valid, but I don't use the word to imply that my experience is in any way equivalent to what others endure.

I'm aware now that there are proper technical terms for what I experienced. Burnout. Chronic stress. Cognitive dissonance. Arguably even post-traumatic stress. When I began to hear the stories of others in similar situations, I connected the dots in my own experience. But those realizations came much later. At the time, all that was apparent was an ever expanding list of physical symptoms. Overwhelming fatigue, changes to my digestion, my sleeping patterns in disarray, my ability to fight off and recover from illness limited. A body completely out of balance, a nervous system permanently stuck in danger mode, never allowing me to rest. The interaction and overlap of these issues with anxiety, depression and hypothyroidism made understanding my body a complete minefield. I felt like a vicious circle trapped inside a vicious circle. Shalom was a distant dream.

This isn't the fallout for everyone that doubts, but for me, the dissonance overflowed from my heart and mind into my muscles and limbs. My body was unable to resolve the crisis. I embodied the trauma of doubt. Unaware of what was happening to me, unable to listen to my body, there is no denying that my coping mechanism of constant distraction added substantial fuel to the fire. Never stopping, always distracting, keeping busy to keep my mind at bay and never allowing silence all served to confirm my body's worst suspicions. I was under attack and had to stay alert to keep myself safe.

When it reached the point that the fatigue was so bad that I couldn't walk upstairs without resting half way, I sought medical help and was eventually diagnosed with Chronic Fatigue Syndrome. It made sense, the way it was explained to me is that the root problem with Chronic Fatigue Syndrome is that your body loses its ability to ever go into rest mode. You are constantly stuck in your fight or flight response, waiting for a tiger to pounce. When asked whether anything had occurred in my life that might have caused my body to feel threatened, I was uncharacteristically honest with the consultant and explained more about my life than most of my friends knew. Her official diagnosis was that the enduring emotional turmoil caused by my doubt had led to the CFS and that I wouldn't get physically better until I could resolve my questions. CFS is such a misunderstood illness that for the sake of any fellow sufferers, I will gently point out that it is a complex diagnosis which causes multiple problems. It doesn't always have emotional trauma, or anything definite at all as the catalyst. Don't interpret or judge anyone else's experience through the lens of mine.

I'm not sure whether CFS was an appropriate diagnosis, or whether it was a way to deal with me in a system that isn't set up to deal with the physical effects of an existential crisis. I'm not a doctor or a trauma informed therapist. The point is that whatever the correct diagnosis, my daily reality was impacted in the same way: a dysregulated nervous system.

Physical health, mental health, doubt. I added another label to my collection of problems and felt completely trapped, unsure how I would ever escape. My trust in my body reached rock bottom.

Fulfillment

They have forsaken me,
the spring of living water,
and have dug their own cisterns,
broken cisterns that cannot hold water. Jeremiah 2.13

As the years progressed, it became increasingly difficult to carry on with my tactic of avoid and suppress. My body was sending me clear messages in every possible way that I was not okay. Life felt empty. It is widely established that the first step in overcoming an issue is to acknowledge it in the first place, and I was beginning to crumble under the pressure of avoiding the problem. But that didn't stop me from trying. I dug countless wells and cisterns to try and find my own source of water, trying to sidestep the issue by managing perfectly well without God. For nearly a decade after the worship conference, I darted from one cistern to another, never stopping to consider their worth. They were a step up from the white noise of my normal distractions; it was a replacement that I was after rather than something to take my mind off things. I was desperate to find something which could fill the hole within me, something which could bear my weight. Fulfillment and wholeness. My life became so cluttered by the presence of these endeavors that

I had no energy to confront my doubts, which I suppose was the point.

The biggest way that I tried to meet this need was by living a productive, organized, Instagram worthy life. I wanted my life to feel perfect, mended and fixed. Maybe if I had a clean and tidy house, it would make up for the fact that my head was such a mess. Maybe if I made sure every area of my life was completely controlled, it would replace the need for anything spiritual. Maybe if I excelled at every hobby that I tried my hand at, that would prove to me that I was enough. I hoped that this lifestyle might offer me satisfaction and make me feel complete. Adding fuel to the fire in this area was the fact that I am a perfectionist. It was already my tendency to try and oversee and control every aspect of my life. I also recognize now that deep perfectionism is partly to blame for why I reacted so badly to doubt. Because my faith wasn't perfect, I thought that I had failed. Not a feeling I deal well with.

Another tactic that I attempted was to try and fix my physical and mental health issues in isolation to my doubts. Perhaps I could bypass the need to resolve my questions and carry on with life regardless. Refusing to accept doubt as the root cause of my problems, I tried to cure my anxiety and fatigue by eating well, exercising and meditating. This is an opaque area, as obviously it is important to look after your physical and mental wellbeing and some of these practices can be incredibly healing. There is no denying that a healthy lifestyle benefited me in many ways. In my lowest moments, meditation and yoga kept my head above water, and they are habits that I continue to this day. The issue was that I approached them with unattainable expectations. I hoped that yoga and mindfulness might offer me the lasting peace that I so desperately craved. That eating healthily might override the pain I felt in my body, or maybe even cure me. I placed my hope in cisterns that couldn't hold water. For no matter how often I meditated or how many vegetables I ate, the impact of doubt was not abated.

Inevitably, the wells and cisterns began to lose their varnish. A clean house was nice to live in but didn't make my mind feel any less fraught. Yoga was undeniably good for me, giving my muscles strength and helping to regulate my nervous system, but it couldn't go far enough to address the root problem. I was forced to acknowledge the issue. Doubt refused to be ignored. Something needed to change.

* * *

You find yourself stuck in quicksand. Sinking. You try to find something to hold onto, something to pull you to safety. You desperately grab anything within reach that appears robust and secure. You run out of logs, branches and twigs; they appeared strong, promised hope, but sank under your weight. Frantic, you twist and turn, not willing to give up, whilst realizing that there is nothing you can do to escape. You cannot save yourself. Eyes straining, you see someone standing nearby, on solid ground. Holding a lifebelt. This is it, your only chance. The man moves to throw the ring, and you realize that all you need to do is stop straining, surrender and lift your arms so that the man can aim and the ring can go over your head. The rescue is there, but you have to accept it. You have to accept grace.

The aim is true. You are still stuck in the quicksand, with all the fear, tension and mess that brings. But now you have a rock solid ring around you to lean on, with the promise that one day you will be pulled to safety. Your future is secure.

You aren't likely to recognize the promise and hope that the man holds until you've got to know him a bit. You aren't even likely to accept the ring until you trust the person throwing it and can be sure that he isn't another false hope. Take a look. Find out if he is trustworthy. If he can take your weight.

Small threads of faith

Looking back at those first years of doubt is like watching a roller coaster with a fault. Twisting and turning, up and down, but every so often simply stuttering to a complete halt with the occupants left dangling mid-air.

The full speed, adrenaline high phases were marked by desperate, feverish searching. Recognizing that I couldn't keep avoiding the problem, I went to the other end of the extreme, believing that I needed to do more, learn more and find a way to convince myself into faith. I was propelled forwards by the mistaken belief that I could find faith simply by working out the right answers. I thought that I could override doubt with knowledge. It hadn't worked up to that point in my life, but perhaps I just needed to find better, cleverer answers. I hoped that faith was something I could achieve once I was able to jump through all the right hoops and tick all the right boxes.

The highs were matched in their intensity only by the depression and anger that I felt when things seemed to reach a full stop. When the fight left me and all hope of progress was lost. Questions of whether I was doing it wrong, thoughts of whether I was simply not chosen or wanted tormented me. Long periods of nothingness, stretches of time filled with distraction and avoidance.

I was stuck on this temperamental ride for years, pushed between the two options by fear and disappointment. I was unable to see another way, and found myself trapped within the impossibility that I believed the answer to my doubt lay outside of what I already felt and knew, but that it was within my own power and responsibility to sort it out.

It's worth noting that during these times, suggestions and implications that doubt was a season that would be experienced and moved on from in a simple, linear fashion were extremely damaging. More on that later.

Once several years had passed with nothing much changing, I tried to change tack again. I accepted that I simply couldn't carry on as I was. My body and mind were cracking beneath me. So instead of flooding myself with what other people thought about God, I tried, for the first time in my life, to make my faith my own. I allowed myself space to wonder whether it was simply fear that drove me, or whether I could find within myself anything that pointed me to God.

My tactic changed from searching for an instant fix to focusing on a gradual, steady, sustainable rebuilding. The image I use to think about this approach to faith is a circle made up of crisscrossing threads, built up one strand at a time. Each strand represents an individual considered conclusion or opinion about God, or at least something that points me towards God. A small but significant thread of faith. Unless the circle eventually becomes covered in threads, it will always remain quite a fragile thing, but it is at least tangible, something to see, something to physically hold on to. If one thread snaps in the future, the others will remain secure, there is no need for the whole thing to unravel. They are separate hard fought fragments, pinpricks in the dark that let in cumulative light but are not dependent on each other. Resilience is integral.

Tied round a ring, small threads of faith,

a cliff on which to hold.
Fragile alone but as they join,
together form a whole.
The hope, the desperate maybe,
for a rock beneath my feet.
Restore the foundation that so
accidentally unraveled.

Yes, I actually used an embroidery hoop to make the idea a reality, and as I got out a pile of old threads to use as the strands, I realized that holding that tangled mess of threads in my hand was the closest thing to hope I had felt for a long time. The hope that these threads would find a place on the hoop, representing future faith. The hope of faith restored, or possibly discovered for the first time.

The threads that I discovered over the years that followed are scattered throughout the rest of the book. Some significant, some more tenuous, held together they started to give me what I had never had before: my own story.

April 2015

Self-awareness is a double-edged sword. The ability to diagnose my problems and interpret my own life brings issues as well as rewards. Ignorance would definitely be preferable sometimes. I've realized that my life seems to have narrowed into two different states of being, modes that are determined by how heavily things weigh on me and how much optimism I can muster.

Mode one. Roller-coaster highs. Active searching. The "it's real but I just need to work harder to find it" mentality. Basically another way of saying intentional, prolonged vulnerability and pain. A desperate attempt to hold onto hope. Heartbreak appears to be inevitable. I fall prey to every thoughtless comment, every empty word, the fake smiles and polished teeth that pop Christianity has to offer, bearing no resemblance to my actual life. This level of resilience is almost impossible to maintain, and its failure is not just a disappointment to me but to all those around me. Slip out of this mode and people very quickly run out of things to say. You can't help someone who doesn't want to be helped.

But inevitably the ride begins to slow. Progress stalls and takes me down into anger. Mode two. The growing threat of bitterness. It's real but unattainable. I'm not wanted, too broken. Why? I am barely surviving; what lessons will be learnt if the pressure becomes too much? I don't treat strangers like this, let alone friends, and I am supposed to be an inherently flawed human. Ironically, I probably have more self-respect in this state than the others. The anger is fueled by the sense that I don't deserve to be treated like this. How do I continue without my view of God becoming irreparably damaged?

I waver between these states, unable to find a middle ground. No straight line in between the roller-coaster curves on the graph. To give up seems an impossibility. I am trapped. Whether that is driven by fear or faith is a mystery. How do I find a compromise, an escape from this cycle? Is there any way out of this that allows me to keep a foot in the door to faith without destroying my own heart?

Small thread of faith: look up

Needle threaded, hoop ready. Well, actually this isn't a thread. This is what I slowly crunched out of my old-fashioned label maker to stick onto the inner circle of my embroidery hoop of faith. Even if the worst were to happen and all the threads snapped, this truth will always remain. It is the reason that I haven't walked away, the reason that my stubborn soul has clung on.

Sat here at my desk, I can close my eyes, listen to the birds and feel quite still. But the reality is that I am spinning on the Earth's axis at about 600 miles per hour, whilst simultaneously orbiting the sun at about 67,000 miles per hour. All while floating on a green and blue ball in space.

It is very easy to pay no attention to this reality. The way we structure our lives around us seems intentionally designed to narrow our experience, to stop us from contemplating the bigger questions. Consumed by the mundane, focused exclusively on the reality that we have constructed for ourselves, the systems and rhythms of life, we seem to have lost the ability to remember the bigger picture. Or maybe it is just me.

My absolute rock bottom, the thing that seems to be unbreakable within me and the thing that I can't talk my way out of even on days when the doubt is overwhelming is the feeling

I get when I look up. When I consider the universe, the earth, the stars, the unfathomable vastness of it all. When I picture the earth, teeming with the impossibility of abundant life. I zoom out in my mind, shift my perspective up above the earth to see us hanging there in space like a marble, and it makes me feel dizzy enough to knock a sense of reality back into me. It shocks me. The impact it has on me is so strong that I can even remember the first time that it happened, sat in a Physics lesson as a teenager. It has made it to such an important position on my hoop because it serves as my safety net. I think it would be impossible to overstate how important it is for me to know that however far I fall, so far, this thought has always caught me.

It is accompanied by the realization that we can never start our questioning from a neutral standpoint. I didn't realize that I saw things through a lens, a worldview. I was arrogant enough to think that I was immune. But of course I do, and my lens seems to be particularly skeptical, bordering on materialistic. I struggle to accept that there is another dimension to life. Perhaps that's why the dizzy feeling is significant. By itself, it doesn't constitute faith or bring me closer to God, but the shift in perspective jolts me out of my comfort zone and creates the nagging feeling that there might be more to life than my daily structures lead me to believe. When I find myself thinking that it's all too good to be true and too far-fetched, looking up and considering the reality of our situation reminds me that it's already too good to be true. It's already absurd. We are spinning on a rock in space.

Small thread of faith: longing

Remember how the LORD your God led you all the way in the wilderness these forty years, to humble and test you in order to know what was in your heart, whether or not you would keep his commands. Deuteronomy 8.2

Forty years (or over a decade) in the desert. Wilderness wanderings. A time of testing. Comforts and structures destroyed, their power revealed as meaningless. Not strong enough to take your weight. A time of anger, despair and confusion, but also a chance to discover what your priorities are. What actually matters. To find out what is in your heart.

My expectation was that the longer my period of doubt carried on, this time of desert exposure, the easier it would be to walk away. That the desire would ebb and that I would simply move on with my life and forget about it. Having been raised in a Christian home, I always had the unspoken suspicion that any faith I had wasn't really my own. That once removed from situations where it was being reinforced, it might simply dissipate.

It has been a real surprise to find that isn't the case. Underneath the anger, the pain and the exhaustion, the truth that I can't deny is that I desire God. That there is something captivating about Jesus that I can't escape. That there must be more to life. No matter how bad the doubt has been, I have never stopped hoping that it is all true. This season has left me raw and bruised, but also clearer. Refined. Being in the desert has left me desperate to find water, water that will truly quench my thirst.

Perhaps it is all just driven by fear. Fear of death, fear of hell, fear of an empty and meaningless existence. But it doesn't feel totally like fear. It feels like hunger. Longing. Reading through the gospels provokes a feeling of deep yearning and jealousy in me. I want to be there. I want to meet this man. I feel inexplicably drawn to his words. His reactions and responses continually surprise me and keep me going back for more.

This sense of longing is not a unique experience; many across the centuries have found within their hearts this desire for God. You need look no further than the Psalms for corroboration, where the longing for God is compared to the need for life sustaining water. The Psalms frame longing as a matter of life or death, and I don't think that the writers were being overdramatic.

The significance of unearthing this sense of longing within my own soul cannot be overstated. It marked a turning point. A ray of clarity in the messy, clouded, overwhelm of doubt. It was a shift towards actively trying to sort through my questions. Longing combined with the recognition that I couldn't find any kind of sufficient replacement for God gave me drive, a reason to try. For the first time in years, it felt like something had come into focus. We will come to my sorting out in good time, but please allow me a diversion. For doubt cannot be dealt with in isolation. At some point, for most people, doubts are voiced and lives are lived in community. After years of enduring doubt, it is no surprise that I have a few things to say about how to make these conversations and relationships helpful, on a personal and institutional level.

Part II

On Friends and Church

Start here

If you are privileged enough to have a friend open up to you about their doubts, congratulations. You must have demonstrated something that has made you seem safe, trustworthy and wise. But a word of warning: consider how important this is. An offer of vulnerability and honesty is a sacred moment, not one to be taken lightly.

Just a note on the opposite scenario. If you have a friend who hasn't opened up to you, don't take it personally. It could be for any number of reasons and doesn't mean that you are not trusted. I have some marvelous, wise, kind and sensitive friends who have patiently walked beside me, unafraid of my questions, allowing me the space to be completely honest. But I also have some equally marvelous friends that I haven't shared these things with. Initially, the reason for this was deeply embedded with shame. I lost the nerve to be honest and felt too embarrassed to admit that I had effectively been living a double life. Every negative interaction that I had reinforced the fear that opening up would put precious friendships at risk and seriously damage the way that people saw me. And although this part of my life is no longer a secret, hidden away in shame, there are still some friends that I don't really talk about it with. It's not due to a lack of trust, or the fear that they would disown me, it's more to do with the simple fact that it's an exhausting thing to talk about every time you meet someone for coffee.

Back to that moment of admission. I suggest that before reacting, the first step is to try and put yourself in their shoes. What might run through your head once those words are out of your mouth? An internal monologue that might include thoughts like this:

Will they judge me? Disown me? Hate me?

Please let them say something that fixes this/Please let them listen without trying to fix me.

Please let them have the answers that I desperately need/ Please let them just sit with me.

If they don't know what to say, will it make things awkward?

If I don't make any progress, will they give up on me?

Will they ever speak to me again?

Will they tell people?

Will they see me as fragile, vulnerable, a liability?

Will it stain our friendship and put it out of balance?

What if they say something that makes it worse?

Will my faith become dependent on them?

I don't know what I want or need from this, but I can't keep it hidden any longer.

There is no denying that these conversations are hard. But we have to consider the alternative. Simply avoiding the conversation altogether is not a viable option. Ignoring the problem does not make doubt fade away. Instead, the questions multiply, fed and powered by feelings of pain, anger and bitterness. They become a black hole within you, threatening to suck more of your life into the darkness. Mental health may begin to suffer. These are big questions, with big implications, and it can feel as though your very identity is under the spotlight. If you have nowhere to turn to and no one to talk to, then leaving the building, leaving the community and self-preservation by ignoring the doubts altogether become enticing options.

These conversations are vital. Holy. But fraught with the possibility of pain and embarrassment. Once you understand that and the importance of the conversation that is unfolding, you are ready to think about your response.

Things that someone struggling with doubt might not want to hear

Have you tried praying? But I mean, really praying?

Have you tried praying on your knees?

You just need to read the Bible more.

Have you read the Psalms?

God has sent this suffering to mold you and make your faith stronger.

God doesn't give you more than you can handle.

I'm sure underneath it all you are still saved.

I think you are purposefully holding yourself back.

You must be doing it wrong.

Have you cried out to God?

Are you hiding some terrible sin?

Maybe just a few medium sins then?

I know exactly what you are going through.

Everything happens for a reason.

You will be grateful for this time in the long run.

You just need to open your heart and ask God into your life, it's simple.

I hope that reading through this list has filled you with horror. I hope you can see how damaging it could be if any one of these sentences formed part of someone's response. And they aren't hypothetical or made up, they are all things that have been said to me, either in person or in some form of general advice for doubters.

I accept that the correct title for this section should really be "Things that I don't want to hear." I can only speak from my own experience so the list will always be subjective. But the reason for being argumentative about it is to make two points. One: however well-meaning you are, don't step in to try and fix things before you have taken the time to understand the situation. You run a high risk of doing more harm than good and the assumptions and judgments might also make it less likely that the person struggling will be willing to let someone else in. Remember the example of Job's friends, who started off on a good track by simply listening but quickly veered off in the wrong direction. While we are talking about fixing things, consider whether that is your place, or whether that is even what your friend is asking for. Manage expectations and gently set boundaries. Of all the people I have spoken to, I have only ever asked for direct help from three, and two of those people were church leaders. With the others, all I was asking for was support. Love. Cake. Help to sort through my thoughts. I was not their responsibility to mend, the pressure of that would have been too much at both ends.

And two: don't assume that the person hasn't already tried everything that you are suggesting. After years of a serious struggle with doubt, I get fed up of people suggesting that I might like to try praying or reading the Bible. Or that I'm not crying out to God quite loudly enough, or in the right physical position. It can feel as though people are trying to fob me off with platitudes rather than actually listen to what I have to say. If what you say isn't based on your own experience and you are simply saying the first thing that comes to mind to try and escape the conversation as quickly as possible, please read on.

Don't make empty promises

Don't promise to support someone, or even simply pray for someone, if you have no intention of following through. If you don't know what to say, don't jump from cliché to cliché, signpost the person on to someone else.

Above all, don't say nothing. I have had friendships dwindle over the years, not through arguments or disagreements about my questions, but simply through trusting people enough to finally open up to them, only for them to never mention it again. I was honest, but they didn't know what to say, so they said nothing at all. At least Job's friends stuck around, even if they did get the wrong end of several sticks.

It's not only the instant dismissal. There is another category of saying nothing: simply running out of steam. Suggestions and conversation exhausted, with doubt becoming the proverbial elephant in the room. I suspect that this situation arises from expectations and roles being wrong on either or both sides. If the goal has been to fix things, then conversations can become painfully challenging if you can't seem to follow the expected linear line between doubt and faith. Friendship is not stamped out, but begins to suffocate in the awkwardness.

This is another moment to swap places, so that you can try to imagine the impact of this slow fading. It might be confirmation of your friend's worst suspicions: they might think themselves unsalvageable and beyond help. Please don't misunderstand the tone of this, I appreciate that it's hard. If problems aren't resolved by prayer ministry, through reading a few self-help faith books or by listening to some clever apologetics, we don't have the tools to take things further. Doubt not being openly discussed within normal congregational settings impacts the supporter as well as the doubter. With no examples to follow, no appropriate resources to hand and perhaps no experience in dealing with anything similar, it's no wonder that communication gets messy.

* * *

On one of the first occasions that I opened up to someone, it was as though they couldn't hear the words I was saying. Not acknowledged in any way, simply ignored. I would have laughed from the shock had it not been such an awful moment. I had the image in my head that I was stood in front of them, holding my heart out on a plate, only for them to completely disregard it. As I relived the moment later that day, the image shifted to a man walking towards me as I stood, still holding my heart out on a plate. As he reached me, he knelt and took what I was offering. I will return to this later, but for now, let me say that I find it hard to believe that my brain, with its self-confidence in shreds, could make up an image that gave me such worth.

Don't rush

There is another type of response to admissions of doubt that is so nuanced that it deserves its own section. The "yes, but not yet" category. Statements such as these:

Doubt is a healthy part of faith.

Doubt will refine your faith and make it deeper.

Doubt is a sign of maturing faith.

Doubt is a doorway to spiritual growth.

There is no denying that those statements can be true, and that (spoiler alert) eventually, they were for me. But the nuance is contained within the word eventually. In my early days of doubt, days marked with fear, desperation and a deep loss of identity and security, doubt was not welcome, nor did it feel in any way beneficial to my faith. Maybe the misunderstanding stems from issues of definition. If by doubt you mean a question about the interpretation of a particular passage of scripture that leads to a deeper understanding of God, then of course these statements apply. But when you use doubt to mean the total collapse of faith, the statements taste sour. Doubt had opened a doorway that I wished I could slam shut. These phrases were so far from the truth that the suggestion and comparison that I could and should be using my doubt for growth made my questioning into something else that I felt like I was failing at. I couldn't even manage to doubt properly.

This is the perfect example of the impact that it has when people gloss over the darkest moments in their testimonies about doubt. Trying to follow these examples pressurized me to rush past the pain and push through the experience as quickly as possible. The truth was that I needed to do the exact opposite. I needed to sit with it. Embrace and admit the heartbreak, rather than suppress my emotions once again to please those trying to help me and avoid being seen as a bad doubter. If I had rushed past those early years of doubt, never letting myself fully feel the sense of loss and separation, I might never have unearthed the longing for God which allowed me to move forward. Doubt can only refine and strengthen your faith if your heart has integrity. If you have the courage to be honest with yourself. Although the wounds are deep, don't rush people past the pain.

The best way that I can think of to describe this process is that doubt opened up cracks which, over time, allowed faith to seep deeper. I prefer this to pictures of doorways because it doesn't diminish the havoc and pain of the cracking. It implies causality without suggesting that the scars automatically disappear or become less painful once faith matures. The Japanese art of kintsugi, where broken pieces of pottery are mended with gold captures this idea perfectly. The cracks are left visible, seams of gold tracing the scars, often resulting in a more beautiful piece of pottery than before the breakage occurred. Have a look on the internet if you don't believe me.

It is a natural response to try and fix pain. We want to be able to help each other, to provide comfort and hope. But instead of running the risk of offering empty words and meaningless or damaging clichés, sometimes the most meaningful thing that we can do for each other is to simply offer our presence. To be willing to wait in the uncomfortable, unresolved middle of our stories.

Things that someone struggling with doubt might want to hear

Doubts are normal.

Questions don't mean you have failed.

I'm listening.

We love you.

You are still included and welcome.

You still count.

How you are feeling matters.

You are not a burden.

Doubt doesn't define you.

I don't know why this is happening.

I hope this makes it clear which ballpark you should be in. One of kindness, respect, and safety. For unless someone feels safe, then conversations about doubt are very unlikely to be helpful. The fight/flight/freeze response is not conducive to honesty. Maybe it helps to think of it this way: when one of my children hurts themselves, my reaction isn't to tell them off, or that it was their fault, or that it will teach them a useful lesson. What I aim to do is to acknowledge their pain and offer comfort. The same applies to doubt.

Infectious

There is a different side to this which can't be ignored. Perhaps when these conversations go wrong, it is caused by the fear of doubt being infectious. That even listening to someone express their questions will cause them to transfer and open an unwanted doorway. If this fear response sounds familiar, turn back a page or two. Doubts are normal. Questions don't mean you have failed...

The threat of infection is two-sided. I am well aware that I pose a risk. The way that I manage that risk seems to depend on who I am talking to. With some people, I tell myself that I can't talk to them about my deepest thoughts because I don't want to infect them with my doubt. They are too pure, too unburdened. It would ruin them to even consider the things that I think about. What a judgment of their faith.

The flip side: with other people, I want to throw questions into conversations which are designed to stop them in their tracks. I want to infect them. Maybe it stems from the deep need of company, or maybe it's because I can't believe that they could have a faith so strong that it wouldn't be called into question if they experienced what I have. I presume that they haven't thought things through properly.

Arrogant judgment and malicious jealousy: neither a healthy

place to stand.

To give a fair account of myself, those are the extremes. I don't pick one of those options for everyone that I meet. And the desire to infect has never actually resulted in action. I am non-confrontational to my very core. My normal reaction, as a people pleaser, is to say absolutely nothing at all, for fear that they will never speak to me again.

The years I spent trying to steal a sense of faith from other people has polluted my opinion of myself and others. I assume that people with faith have attained something that I can't reach, have progressed further with their thinking, are generally just better, cleverer, less broken human beings. That's where the jealousy comes in, the desire to knock them down a rung or two so that I don't feel so inadequate. The other approach comes from the arrogant conclusion that it's the other way round; it isn't that I haven't progressed far enough, it's that I've gone too far, too deep. I view others as further down the ladder, and I don't want to pull them up to my height for fear that they will get dizzy and fall off. The combination of low self-worth and an attitude of constant comparison has made me a prickly beast, prone to judge and misinterpret everyone I meet.

Despite the mess that I seem to work myself into on this issue, the bottom line is that describing doubt as infectious is the wrong way to look at it. Fear has blurred our vision. Sharing doubts or questions may well make the person on the listening end confront problems that they had not considered before, but we don't need to view it as transmitting an illness. Doubt shouldn't be seen as a disease, its sufferers afflicted by some horrible malady, and it shouldn't have the same debilitating impact, even if it sometimes does. We need to find a way out of this way of thinking. In case I haven't made my opinion clear, doubts are not something to be feared. Doubts are normal. Questions don't mean you have failed.

Doubt friendly

The rest of this section has been concerned with the personal level, talking about doubt in one to one conversations. Allow me to widen the lens for a moment and consider the bigger picture, opening up the conversation to a corporate level by making churches more doubt friendly spaces.

You may wonder why I care, but it would be a mistake to assume from what you have read so far that I have given up on church. Despite all that I have experienced, I still attend church. Within its walls I have found some of my dearest friends. It has always lured me in with its promise of community. However, I accept that what I've said within these pages betrays my disappointment with the church. When the connections haven't gone far enough, when conversations have ended in awkward and painful silence. At its worst, doubt made me feel like I didn't belong, and I struggled to find anything within the walls of church that managed to convince me otherwise. It felt like I had lost my place. I'm well aware that for some, this is more than just a feeling, with doubts and questions leading to confused and hurt people being overtly shown the door.

Although I do not blame myself in any way for my doubts, I do accept partial responsibility for the wall of silence that I experienced in church, simply because for years, I did nothing to break the cycle. I had never heard a story like mine told from the front of church, a story of difficult, wrestling, doubtful faith, so I wasn't brave enough to share mine. The cycle repeats. Sitting silently in the pews affected not just me, but also those sat next to me and those hovering at the door. The problem with this silence is that it does nothing to silence the doubts. They will continue to form, but people will not expect them. They will not have the framework or experience to deal with them. Shame and fear will grab a foothold. The cycle repeats.

I am not ordained. I have no training in theology, church leadership or pastoral care. I worked at a church for less than a year, over a decade ago. I am in no position to offer a comprehensive guide to making churches more doubt friendly places, just as I can offer no step-by-step guide to walking through doubt. But my experience has led me to believe that there are some sensible starting points. Small shifts and changes which could begin the process of balancing the narrative and reducing the stigma and fear that clouds doubt for so many. And I don't want doubt to hog the limelight. The following suggestions apply in equal measure to all of the difficulties that we face in life but which are not often overtly visible in church, including suffering, enduring illness, anger, bereavement, mental health problems, addiction, debt, divorce, eating disorders and miscarriage. The list could go on. All of these experiences need an appropriate place within church, because however uncomfortable it might make us, they could all form a part of the stories of the people sat in the pews. Avoiding them is not only unsustainable, but risks creating a total disconnect from the reality of life. Whatever denomination or expression of church you find yourself in, surely the universal bottom line should be that churches are places of refuge. Places of love and community where we can be honest no matter the topic. Where we can show up with our whole selves and whole lives.

Sharing stories like mine in church is the obvious starting

point for redressing the balance. One of the most crushing parts of my early days of doubt was the isolation. "Is it just me?" was a question that played on repeat in my mind. Finding others, often in books, who felt the same and expressed the same questions gave me validation and connection; significant factors in my movement forwards. But one off sermons, although important, are not sufficient. What is needed isn't just an occasional nod, but a cultural shift. We need sustained vulnerability. We need to be intentional about giving space to the mess. Life laid bare (with appropriate measures and safeguarding in place, of course). We also need to be more specific. Specific when we talk about vague problems and issues that the congregation might be battling through. Specific when we offer pastoral support, rather than a blanket catch all which threatens to catch none. It's very easy to sit in the pews, believing that your thoughts and problems are darker and deeper than those being mentioned if details in others' testimonies are not specified. Naming our problems, in a safe way, not just for the sake of it, but as part of a genuine, all in community, reduces stigma, lessens fear and breaks the cycle of shame for the next person.

It also strikes me that church does a very good job of welcoming questions and wrestling from new Christians, or those considering Jesus for the first time. A common strategy to attract people into church seems to hinge on getting people to ask questions and think about the big issues of life. The problem is that that acceptance doesn't seem to last once people commit. Questions are renamed as doubts, holy wrestling is reframed as a problem. The implication, whether it is intended or not, is that once you have committed, questions should be few and far between. Acceptance of doubts, disagreements and questions don't seem to translate into the normal church service, where the unspoken assumption is that to belong, you need to agree with everything that is said from the pulpit. The only remedy for this is a top down shift in thinking; one that acknowledges that doubts and questions should be accepted and honored at all ages and stages of faith.

Please remember my disclaimer from the prologue. None of this is meant as an attack and neither is it linked to just one church. Ultimately, the reason that I raise it is because I care about church. I don't want to do this alone. I want and need a community. A place at a shared table. But unless the invite to the meal widens, unless the implied conditions (the dress code, the mess code, the positivity code) are dropped, then I fear that empty seats will become more numerous.

Hypocrite

Something which might come as a surprise is that throughout those first few years of doubt, I didn't stop attending church. Leaving was bigger than a personal decision. But the benefit of hindsight has led me to conclude that it might have been healthier in the long run for me to take a break. There are several reasons that those Sunday mornings are marked with pain in my memory, which you might have fathomed from the previous few pages, but one of the most damaging factors was that each and every week, I felt like I was living a lie. Liturgy, prayers, confession, absolution, communion; all the trimmings of an Anglican service made me feel like a fraudulent imposter. Worst of all was the worship music. Given my history with leading worship, it is perhaps understandable that this was a particularly painful part of the service for me. But aside from my personal connection, the truth is that in the vast majority of songs, there was no way that I could sing the words without feeling like a hypocrite. Cryptic and fleeting allusions to rain and storms didn't go quite far enough to make me feel included. I couldn't sing without the niggling thought in my head that pretending I meant the words would make God angrier with me than he clearly already was. Very rarely did the songs reflect my experience of life, faith or God. I hear how that sounds, the church consumer, verging on selfish. But it's not that I am asking for doubt to be mentioned in every song, or every aspect of a service. I simply needed, then and now, for there to be more balance.

In the Psalms, the prayer book of the Bible that has inspired countless songs across the centuries, a significant percentage of the verses can be categorized as lament. Compare that to our modern day Psalter, the top ten or even top hundred worship songs, sung in any given church on any given Sunday, and the disparity is clear. Lament, frustration, anger, questioning; all appear at worst missing, or at best sporadic, in our corporate expression of worship. Not only does this exclude an important theme from the Bible, ignoring the experience of Jews and Christians across the centuries, but for people like me, it can create an atmosphere that is so different from our lived experience that we are left struggling to find our place.

* * *

Music has always been an important part of my life. For someone who is sometimes unable to express my thoughts to others, or even to myself, music gives me a voice. Classic catharsis, playing music has always been a coping mechanism for me, a way to release the pressure, the build-up of emotion within me. To have that ability stripped away at church, at a time when the residual build-up was unbearable, was extremely painful. I lacked the words to grieve my loss of faith. I lost the feeling that I was being supported and raised up through the voices of others.

During one of my lowest moments, a moment where I was left dangling mid-air on the roller coaster, I took a long train journey from one end of England to the other. I never sleep well before a journey, my mind whirling with arrangements, back up plans and the ironic fear of over sleeping. Sat on the train, half asleep, a song appeared, almost fully formed in my head. It's not really even fair to say that I wrote it; it felt more like I was eavesdropping on someone else's performance, quickly scribbling down the notes of what I heard, worried that I wouldn't remember it. Never before has a song come to me like that.

I finally had words to sing and say which were honest. I could express how I felt without being a hypocrite (which sometimes meant leaving out the first half of the repeated refrain). It was such a bizarre experience that I had to wonder whether God himself had given me the words I needed to express my pain, anger and doubt. More on that later, but perhaps the biggest clue comes from the words themselves. The ending does the exact thing that I find difficult about the Psalms, it shifts to the positive. Given how uncomfortable that makes me, how likely am I to have contributed to the problem? Maybe they are a lesson. They do shift, they do express hope, but hope of the stubborn variety. A refusal to concede.

Longing for hope instead of despair
Desperate for joy instead of this emptiness
Are you the answer? Are you the cure?
God will you rescue me?

Lord I believe, help my unbelief.

For my soul is thirsty, but my strength has gone
The seed it has broken, securities torn
All that remains is this hunger for you
When will you answer me?

Lord I believe, help my unbelief.

What strength do I have that I should still hope?
Exhausted I'm running, I'm searching for you
How long can I stand here alone and afraid?
Why won't you answer me?

Lord I believe, help my unbelief.

But I will fight darkness, I will fight doubt
Don't have the answers, but still my heart shouts
Will you restore me? Bring me to life?
To whom else would I go?

Lord I believe, help my unbelief.

Job 6.11, John 6.68

Small thread of faith: polluted

I have never found the world a comfortable place to live. It's my lack of off switch, the inability to wrap myself in cotton wool, cozy up and pretend that life is entirely wonderful. I don't often go for a full day without the thought of death giving me a jolt.

For years, I found it easy to use those feelings and my experience of life as fuel to push me further away from God. Christianity presented itself to me as happy, joyful, life is wonderful. Probably because I wasn't mature enough to notice the lament in the Bible or concentrate through all the sermons. I hadn't got round to reading the books of Job and Lamentations. Sin as a personal problem had been made abundantly clear, but the impact of sin on creation and life as a whole wasn't something I had ever really grasped. The result was that I found no correlation to how I saw things at all. I couldn't connect the dots.

During my phases of reading every theological work that I could get my hands on, these feelings began to shift. I started to understand that Christianity wasn't so at odds with this feeling as I had suspected. I began to see how it could account for why I felt so out of place. I realized that the dissonance I felt between the glimpses of beauty and love in the world, compared to the evil and pain, is the very substance of Christian lament, hope and renewal.

I suspect that it took a while to come to this realization because the definition of hope that I had soaked up had sold itself seriously short. I believed that hope was the fluffy, shiny bubble of believing that a polished and perfect life is almost inevitable. Nothing more than spiritual optimism. With this definition, it's no wonder that I felt so hopeless. With anxiety and depression raging in my mind and body, with war, famine and evil never out of the news cycle, it's no wonder that I couldn't summon within me the ability to believe in that kind of happily ever after. It's no wonder that Christianity made me feel suspicious.

Slowly but surely, my understanding of hope has widened. As ever, Jesus sets the example, and his reaction to the pain he encountered on earth serves as a starting point. I have learnt to appreciate that hope is only possible when held together with the mess. That it is the stubborn determination to catch glimpses of purpose in the midst of chaos. The defiant ability to see flashes of beauty and restoration despite having eyes wide open to the fractured world around us.

The world is broken. Polluted. Not how it was meant to be. And at some deep level, I feel that. By itself, this didn't offer me a light bulb moment. But it was still a significant realization; a moment where I discovered within myself and my own experience something which pointed me towards Jesus. And the process was beginning to build. The accumulated threads were beginning to form a fabric.

Part III

Reconstruction

Misinterpretation

Let's go back to the toilet cubicle. Take another look at what went on in that moment. With hindsight, I recognize that the gut wrenching feeling that I attributed entirely to doubt had several other layers to it. Disappointment. Anger. Confusion. The realization that what I thought I had been promised had not materialized. The click that I had waited my whole life for had never come, despite me doing everything that was asked of me. My carefully boxed idea of what God looked like and what life as a Christian looked like was blown wide open. Despite years of searching and years of praying, I had no relationship with God. It felt like I had been sold a lie.

What I thought I had been promised was an idealized, fantasy version of Christianity that had the hard edges and rough truths smoothed over. I expected the best friend portrayed in my childhood picture books. Those books had promised faith that felt like unwavering certainty, with no need for doubts to ever cross my mind; prayer that felt like any other two-way conversation, with reasonable requests granted or at least clearly answered; either to be untouched by suffering or else immune to the pain that it brought, and that God's presence in my life would be tangible and practical, with my every step and decision guided and directed.

With such high expectations, it is no surprise that my faith was too thin to bear the weight of my adult reality. I was 22 years old when things came crashing down and to be frank, looking at the description of what I believed being a Christian looked like, I'm surprised that it took that long.

Although this is clear to me now, I don't blame myself for not realizing it at the time. I wasn't mature enough to realize that the books I had based my idea of God on lacked nuance. I didn't appreciate the depth and breadth of different interpretations and understanding. I was naïve enough to think that I'd simply been presented with the black and white truth and it hadn't worked. Stuck within this narrow view, pure doubt was my only option. And there is no denying that it was the easier option to start with. "You're not there" is arguably easier to handle than "I was wrong."

The question of whether it was misinterpretation or miscommunication is something that I find difficult to address in a healthy and objective manner. Although I attach no blame to any particular person, church or denomination, there is a strong argument that this caricature of Christianity is reinforced by the general type of shallow, pop Christianity that does its best to draw seekers in by offering a curated view of life as a Christian. For me, the early years of doubt were never very far away from bitterness and cynicism. I was prone to nit-pick my way through songs, podcasts and books, on high alert for any phrase that was so enthusiastic in its focus on the positive aspects of Christianity that it bordered on misleading. Toxic positivity. Yet again, the issue of lament, honesty and bearing our wounds openly rears its head.

The deeper level of what went on in that moment only became clear many years later, significantly only once I had acknowledged that my longing for God was not wavering. The glimpses of Jesus I began to get from reading the Bible in a different way didn't match up with what I expected. I began to get suspicious. Adding those factors to the sheer amount of knowledge about theology that I was gaining in my attempt to find faith in books and the stage was set. My doubt became active. It morphed from a cloud of indescribable despair to a driving force. The churning, inescapable sense that the time had come to learn and unlearn. To renew and discard. To let God escape from the boxes that I had constructed for him.

This process of sorting through beliefs and understanding about God is something that Christians have undergone throughout the centuries, on a personal and institutional level. Recently, this process has been coined, at least on a personal level, as deconstruction. Deconstruction can mean different things to different people. So let me be clear. What I mean by deconstruction is that it became necessary for me to dissect my beliefs about God. To pick them apart one by one in order to examine them and clean off any dirt, before reconstructing them into something that looked a lot more like Jesus. For others, the word might mean something different and end with a different result.

The sum of my misconceptions was equal to what life as a Christian actually looked like on a daily basis. The practicalities. What faith meant, how to approach prayer, how to handle suffering and how much to expect God's guidance and presence in my everyday life. These pillars of faith are huge questions which many Christians would answer differently. This made approaching them feel impenetrable. But I had to at least try. It turned out that the reality of Christianity was almost a complete unknown to me.

Deconstruction required stamina and dogged determination. Hopeful, faithful and holy stubbornness. But if it was worth doing, I would do it properly.

Faith: focus

As Jesus was on his way, the crowds almost crushed him. And a woman was there who had been subject to bleeding for twelve years, but no one could heal her. She came up behind him and touched the edge of his cloak, and immediately her bleeding stopped. 'Who touched me?' Jesus asked. When they all denied it, Peter said, 'Master, the people are crowding and pressing against you.' But Jesus said, 'Someone touched me; I know that power has gone out from me.' Then the woman, seeing that she could not go unnoticed, came trembling and fell at his feet. In the presence of all the people, she told why she had touched him and how she had been instantly healed. Then he said to her, 'Daughter, your faith has healed you. Go in peace.' Luke 8.42–48

The definition of faith that I absorbed growing up was one that left no room for doubt. Faith meant certainty. The words were interchangeable. Faith was only real if my relationship with God was as certain and tangible as my relationship with my best friend and I was only saved if I was sure.

It was clear to me from an early age that I didn't feel that way. But that realization came when I still had hope that the missing link would click into place. When it didn't, this seemingly unattainable target meant that any mention of faith or belief was accompanied by a feeling of deep unease. I felt like a fraud, an imposter who didn't meet the required entry standard. I think it was the outward expression of faith in others more than any other factor that was the straw that broke the proverbial donkey at the worship conference. The extraverted, assured, in your face faith that filled the room around me was too much to bear and the energy required to maintain an outward and inward pretense ran out.

Resolving to unpick this definition immediately brought up an uncomfortable question; one that had the potential to call to a halt any further progress. Put simply, if I have to be completely sure, all the time, then I think that counts me out. Even on my better days I can't imagine being so absolute. Does that rule me out? Is the dividing line quite that sharp?

In the same way that I offer my story as a way to give comfort to those who might find themselves in a similar position, there are other authors and thinkers who have done the same for me. Indeed, working my way out of those early years of despair was hugely aided by finding people brave enough to be honest about their own stories. But it is on this issue that I heard the voices of others further along their journey the loudest. Philip Yancey, Rachel Held Evans, Peter Enns, Sarah Bessey; these authors (and undoubtedly many others) voiced the persistent refrain that faith is not the same as certainty. I admit that it took me a long time to hear them, as certainty was the comfort blanket that I sought and the only way I had of understanding faith. But when I found myself far from certainty but still clinging onto faith, I began to listen. Circumstances forced a shift.

Opening up this definition has been hard, and like much meaningful progress in life, it has been slow and is far from complete. It is an impossible question to consider in isolation to my emotions, to the years I spent overcome by the terror of hell and the constantly reinforced belief that I was inferior. It is not a topic that I will ever have objective distance from.

Faith as certainty, ducks all in a row, is a hard baseline to move forward from. But this is where I have got to. Faith as expressed by the woman in Luke 8.42–48, and named as such by Jesus. The picture we get from the Bible doesn't seem to fit the model of faith that we are often presented with. It's not clear whether the woman had ever seen or spoken to Jesus before, and from the details we are given, she doesn't appear to have repented any sin or asked for forgiveness. She hadn't signed a statement of belief and hadn't been checked over to ensure that her understanding of salvation, heaven and hell were deemed correct by her particular denomination. I know I'm being facetious and am superimposing my own culture in an historically inaccurate way, but I hope the point is clear. Instead of certainty, she approached Jesus because she was desperate. Instead of having total assurance and trust, she simply knew that she had run out of other options. She was willing to take a chance, intrigued by what she had heard or seen, captivated by the idea of this strange man.

She demonstrated faith as the decision to take a risk and move towards Jesus.

In the woman's case, it was physical movement. In mine, it is the movement of my whole being; striving to learn more, to see clearer, to catch stronger and more frequent glimpses of this man and to center my life around what I discover. I attributed these qualities in myself to stubbornness; perhaps they need a rebrand as faith. There are many reasons that I feel drawn to this story, but perhaps this is the biggest. I share the desperation, the pain, but I also find myself inexplicably drawn to Jesus. Like a flower seeking the sun. His defiance, his emotion, his responses. I find him compelling and convicting.

This hasn't always been the case. I was too familiar with the surface level and found it too normal and stale to be captivating. I couldn't get past the blond-haired, blue-eyed, nice man of the picture books. It has only been through the process of learning the historical context and delving into theology that I have begun to find Jesus so interesting. Reading through some of Tom Wright's *New Testament for Everyone* series helped to change the gospels from black and white to color. If Jesus were to stand in front of me, there is no doubt that he would have my trust, my allegiance, my love. Is that faith?

I remember presenting a long list of unanswerable questions to an exceptionally wise friend a few years ago (why this, why that, what about cancer, the holocaust). He smiled and said Jesus. I remember being frustrated and thinking that he was purposefully avoiding the questions because he couldn't answer them any more than I could. But perhaps I am beginning to understand why he said what he did. He didn't mean it as a justification, or an answer, or an explanation to my impossible questions. He meant it as his response. As the thing he clings to despite those questions. I'm beginning to understand that faith is the willingness to try and keep Jesus in focus, even when everything else around me blurs.

There is no point pretending that reframing faith in this light is a one-step cure to alleviating doubt. It does nothing by itself to answer my questions, still my fears. It doesn't help me answer the question of whether any of it is actually true. But what it does is offer me a version of faith that allows doubt space. On all but the heaviest days, doubt might make the journey harder and more sluggish, but movement will still be possible. What it does is give me a new approach to faith, and a new way to carry doubt.

* * *

Twelve years is too long to have endured this. Chronic illness. Despised, rejected, feared. No one will come close for fear of being tainted. Any hope of a future stolen.

I have tried everything, done all I can. But I am broken. I

have nothing left. Is it my fault? Did I do something wrong?

And yet.

I have heard rumors of a man. A man who seems to be able to heal people. Maybe if I could get close to him, even just touch his cloak. Would that be enough? Could he truly be that powerful?

Getting anywhere near him will take all the courage I have left. I would have to be in public, in a crowd, push my way to the front. I might touch people, make them unclean. What would they do to me if I were caught?

There is no other option, but is he really worth the risk?

"Daughter. I see you. I notice you. Your faith has healed you."

Prayer: thaw

My expectation of prayer was simple. A conversation. That God would hear me and respond in a way that was clear. I had a picture book that depicted prayer as talking to a friend on the phone and I took that image to heart.

After the toilet moment, I spent years crying out to God, often in the small hours, asking for help. For anything. But nothing ever happened. No tangible sense of peace or love. No reassurance. Just silence and emotional pain strong enough to cause an actual ache in my heart. So I stopped asking, my expectations shattered. Like a sulking teenager holed up in their bedroom, I closed off all communication. Perhaps that analogy is unfair. All I heard was silence and all I heard from other Christians were constant testimonies of feeling God's presence, a deep connection or hearing God speak to them in a variety of ways, particularly at times of distress and difficulty. I wasn't sulking, I was hurt. Confused. I felt completely abandoned. The discrepancy gave my heart another opportunity to believe that I was not wanted, or that I was doing something wrong.

More than any other aspect of faith, prayer is the part that I find the hardest. I simply don't understand it. I admit that listening to other people pray can make me feel at best uncomfortable and at worst angry. In my experience, prayer betrays someone's theology more than people seem to realize and I often find myself wondering whether I have a totally different understanding of God than the people around me. But despite my protests, despite my confusion and anger, the problem I face is that prayer bleeds out of me whether I want it to or not. My soul betrays me. Often my darkest moments, when I feel the furthest from faith, are the times when I produce my most desperate prayers. I can't seem to help myself from directing my thoughts to someone; I can't seem to break the connection. My soul, whether spoken or wordless, demands an audience.

Finding myself unable to make a clean break from prayer has forced me to persevere, but that perseverance has to be balanced with the reality that my heart is extremely vulnerable and the act of meaningful prayer requires that vulnerability to be placed center stage; all comfort blankets and protection thrown off. You see my dilemma.

There is no point pretending that my reconstruction in this area means that I've worked it all out or that I have unlocked the mysteries of prayer. Prayer is a time and a space where heaven and earth interlock. How could we ever hope to understand it? I draw huge (perhaps selfish) reassurance from knowing that prayer seems to be a challenge for people whether they doubt or not. Even a simple internet search on prayer brings up countless podcasts, talks, courses, books and blogs. Prayer causes confusion. We don't find it easy.

So instead of trying to work it all out, all I have tried to do is to reconstruct habits of prayer that allow me to open my heart to God in a way that doesn't do any damage. In a similar way to my evolution with faith, I have tried to widen my definition of prayer. My hesitant desire has led me down the path of different types of prayer. It is the story book, best friend type prayers that cause me the most pain, so I avoid them, individually and corporately. But I have become increasingly comfortable with contemplative silence, meditation on a particular passage, putting myself into the story type prayers. Prayers that take me out of myself. I have also found solace in the prayers of others and in ancient liturgy, new within the old, hope contained within prayers which have been passed down for generations. Don't misunderstand me; even within these prayers, the incessant niggle that I am talking to myself is a constant companion and the issue of what I expect God's response to be is very muddy. The closest I have got to the conversational, prayer request type prayers is to simply allow my mind to wander and my emotions to overflow, without forming anything into words. Allowing God permission to enter and to observe. It's a start.

Prayer is still a live issue for me. I find it difficult. But the bottom line is that these cautious advances all serve the purpose of keeping lines of communication open, but in a way that doesn't do me harm. The way I view it is that I am trying to warm my heart back up again. Those silent nights of despair left me cold and hardened. You don't spread butter straight from the fridge and in a similar way I am trying to thaw slowly, keep momentum going, keep my experience and definition of prayer widening until prayer no longer feels like such a threat to my stability.

* * *

Recognizing the disordered, scattered and messy overflow of my soul as prayer didn't come naturally. Prayer of this type didn't correlate with my expectation of an easy two-way conversation. And naming it as prayer was prompted in part by a surprising source: social media. For better and often worse, social media is a place where people feel able to be honest. In my experience, the relative anonymity seems to make people willing to share things online that they wouldn't necessarily repeat in real life conversations. I follow some incredible accounts, where the wisdom, courage and grace of the human behind the screen is palpable. And I'll take wisdom wherever I can find it. Exposure to different approaches to prayer and reading honest posts and captions about others' experiences and struggles changed my perspective. The wisdom and generosity of these people (particularly David Gate, Joanna Hargreaves and Joy Vetterlein) hasn't just given me a way to slot myself into the story, but the nudge to recognize that I was already taking part. My nighttime groans, my vented anger and confusion, my disruptive by relentless desire for an audience: this is prayer. Echoing the wordless prayers of Romans 8.26, the lament and rage of the Psalms and the indignation of Job, it's not a neat, sanitized or tidy experience, but it is prayer nonetheless.

Suffering: warhorse

My starting point for approaching the question of suffering was this: that suffering was unlikely if I followed God's plan for my life, but that if it did occur, the loving and comforting presence of God would be so overwhelming that the pain would be more than bearable. I thought that being a Christian meant I had a protective force field surrounding me, ready to zap away anything that would harm me, or provide tangible comfort and clear purpose to any suffering that made it through the gaps.

This outlook didn't last long. I swallowed the disappointment, unable (at that point) to work out why I felt so confused, so betrayed. I also grew up. I became more aware of the complexities of other people's lives, as well as suffering on the world stage. Famine, war, death, illness, terrorism, poverty. One of my closest friends died from Leukemia aged 13. I watched the Twin Towers exploding on a TV screen in a shop on my walk home from high school. I was taught, at age 12, to walk with keys between my fingers just in case. My experience and observation of suffering exploded as my grounding and understanding of Christianity's answer to it imploded.

Add to that the fact that at the best of times, I'm the type of person that can't watch the news without crying. I only watch films and read books that don't involve very much jeopardy and absolutely zero gore (which significantly reduces my options). I well up each and every time an ambulance passes me on the street and I cry if I see people taking part in a race for charity, even if I don't know anyone involved. I am proud to be a highly sensitive person and I can see its benefits. But it does mean that I have a very permeable personality, so perhaps I feel the issue of suffering more intensely than other people. The addition of an anxiety disorder probably doesn't help.

My discomfort in this area is not unique: the problem of suffering has plagued humanity for centuries. And like many before me, at times it can feel too high a barrier to cross. The persistent whisper that there is no way to reconcile what we see with what I thought Christianity offered; it's all a lie, so walk away. Regardless of any work I have done to improve my understanding of theodicy, the problem I discovered with that approach is that it doesn't actually help alleviate the suffering. The suffering is there whether you believe in God or not, and if you chose to walk away, you are left with the problem of how to account for your sense of injustice in a world that you have decided has no intrinsic meaning.

How I felt was compounded by the mismatch between my experience of life and what I heard in church, in worship songs and at Christian festivals. It felt like I was being presented with the promise of a happily ever after, one which I found impossible to understand. It slowly began to dawn on me that the tension I felt stemmed from absorbing the belief that if I was a good Christian, good things would happen, and vice versa. And of course, there is no denying that you could easily back that up with countless passages from the Bible. Just take a look at Deuteronomy and Proverbs. Without wishing to take a detour into Biblical interpretation and hermeneutics, I will simply state that although you can find verses to confirm that point of view, you can also find the opposite. Verses which break the connection between suffering as a consequence of personal action. Take Job, Ecclesiastes and Jesus' response to the tower collapse in Luke 13.4. I can't pretend to explain why the Bible contains both sides of the coin, but the important thing it does is give me the nuance that was missing. It allows me to accept that it is not a black and white issue.

My attempt to reconstruct and clean off my understanding of the Christian response to this issue inevitably brought me to Jesus. The way he approached suffering. I'm no biblical scholar, but as far as I can tell, he never refused a request for healing from an individual. Reading through the gospels, it's as though he couldn't help himself. The particular moment that helped me to reconcile my sense of disappointment in this area is Jesus' reaction to Lazarus' death.

> *When Mary reached the place where Jesus was and saw him, she fell at his feet and said, 'Lord, if you had been here, my brother would not have died.' When Jesus saw her weeping, and the Jews who had come along with her also weeping, he was deeply moved in spirit and troubled. 'Where have you laid him?' he asked. 'Come and see, Lord,' they replied. Jesus wept. Then the Jews said, 'See how he loved him!' But some of them said, 'Could not he who opened the eyes of the blind man have kept this man from dying?'*
> John 11.32–37

My problem with suffering is echoed in the response of Mary and some of the Jews: a fraught mixture of faith and indignation. If you'd been here, this wouldn't have happened. So why weren't you here? Why didn't you stop it? And although Jesus' weeping is deeply moving, particularly as he presumably already knew that he would go on to heal Lazarus, it also highlights my main issue: if it makes God that distraught, then why doesn't he always fix it? Not just in the future depicted in Revelation, but now. Heal everyone, eradicate disease, delay that person by a second to avoid that disaster, perform miracles so often that the very fabric of the laws of physics, biology and medicine are completely undone. Why create a world with the possibility of so much horror? Is love really worth that much evil?

I know that I sound impetuous. Like a child pestering their parents with endless questions of why, when they have no hope of understanding the real answers. I know that the world I am asking for would come with some serious strings attached. But the problem is that these things do sometimes happen. Suffering as a direct result of free will and a fallen world would be easier to stomach if miracles never happened. But they do. You hear miraculous stories and celebrate them, while secretly wondering why them and not you, why the storm that diverted off course and the hurricane that didn't, why God intervened then and not now. Despite actively seeking out the answers, I'm yet to hear or read anything that comes close to being a satisfying answer. Probably because the analogy of a small immature child incapable of understanding the deeper answers is a closer reality than I think. Sometimes I wish that the gospels included an account of someone asking for healing that didn't happen, so that we could study Jesus' reaction and response.

I am well aware that part of the problem is my own limited perspective and my warped timeline. That miracles are meant as signposts, not the destination itself. That asking God to save a Christian from a terminal disease could well be met with the response that they have already been saved. A classic example of an intellectually acceptable answer, but not one that is any comfort when you are trying to navigate brutal darkness and pain with no road signs.

But Jesus' response isn't just weeping. Moving though that is, the weeping is preceded by Jesus "deeply moved in spirit and troubled." In the original Greek, the word which is translated into this phrase is associated with a snorting horse rearing up on its two hind legs to prepare for battle. A horse ready for war. The fuller translation shifts the emotion from sympathetic observer to something richer and much more dangerous. It's sadness, distress and pain, but also anger, rage and power. The resolve to take decisive action. Think about what Jesus went on to do in Calvary not long after this event took place. I live close to a racecourse, and I've stood close to horses that are ready to run. I wouldn't want to get in the way of one about to charge.

The image leaves many of my questions unanswered. Suffering is a perennial issue, not one that I can expect to find neat solutions to. As Philip Yancey so aptly captures in the title to his book on the problem of suffering, it is *The Question that Never Goes Away*. But although it doesn't pretend to give me an answer, what it does is to connect on the personal level, something that the clever theological arguments seem to miss. It's not a "there there" pat on the back response. For Jesus to have felt that depth of emotion, we must have a lot more worth than we can possibly imagine. Does it erase the pain of suffering? No. Does it remove my anxiety about terrible things happening? No. Is it an answer that provides total clarity? No. But what it does do, on my good days, is allow me to believe that Jesus cares.

Providence: blooming concrete

And we know that in all things God works for the good of those who love him. Romans 8.28

Everything happens for a reason.
He's got the whole world in his hands.
He's in complete control.
God's got this/you.
Just trust God's timing.

With phrases like this echoing around every church that I have attended, every small group that I have been part of and a significant number of the songs that we sing in church, how could I avoid absorbing the belief that everything that happens is what God wants to happen? That faith gives you access to an ever present helicopter parent or a cosmic personal assistant who micro manages every aspect of your life, whether you ask him to or not? To a point, it is a comforting thought. A get out clause to every situation: well this is awful, but I know God is in control so he must know what he is doing. This must be what is best. When that belief crumbled away, I felt (I think reasonably) terrified. Unprotected. Exposed to the world and all its evil.

The problem was this: I struggled to see the purpose in

the pain. I struggled to reconcile the indiscriminate evil I saw in the world with the sense that God's guiding hand was at work. I couldn't match these ideas up without damaging my understanding of God's character.

The question of God's purpose and action within the world is known as the doctrine of providence. I am abundantly aware that I am crossing a line here and that a huge caveat is necessary. I know that providence has a wide definition and that not all Christians agree on what it means and I am by no means a theologian (for an accessible but thorough introduction to providence from an actual theologian, I'd recommend the chapter on it in *Café Theology* by Michael Lloyd). My foray into this area of theology took me well out of my depth. But it became apparent that it was vital, as the question of God's guidance in my life and as a whole became a real sticking point. Perhaps because it weighed heavily on how I viewed this period in my life. Whether I thought God intended it or was working against it and whether I thought anything good could possibly come from it. People kept trying to reassure me that doubts were a blessing in disguise and that God would deepen my faith and reveal himself to me in new ways. Forced to swallow the idea that everything happens for a reason, I tried to subdue my pain with the comfort that there must be some greater purpose. But with no higher plan presenting itself, the pain refused to be subdued for long. Anger blurred my vision, with the question of God's guidance in my life also inextricably linked with my deep feeling of abandonment.

My reconciliation, or at least my movement towards reconciliation, came from a very unexpected source. Simply walking through my neighborhood; something I do on a daily basis. (Might I remind you to mind the gap: a long time elapsed between these early feelings of betrayal and my attempt to approach the issue.) I am a naturally nosey neighbor and a thorough assessment of everyone else's front yard brings me great joy. But my focus on noticing plants also led me to notice something else: the weeds which grow up through cracks in between stones, in between fences and even up through concrete when there is no soil or nutrition even visible. Over time, I felt myself beginning to respect these plants. Their stubborn will to survive. Their perseverance in less than ideal conditions. I noticed a similar weed in my own garden (one which could have been easily overshadowed by the other, intended plants) a dandelion that survived despite growing up between two paving slabs right next to a drain. Although my initial approach was to try and weed it out, stripping back the leaves and trying to pry down to the root, nothing I did worked. I couldn't stop its growth. I quickly admitted defeat and decided to respect it (and its audacious yellow flower) instead. It became one of the plants that I checked on the most.

My personal opinion (and might I refer you back to the caveat on the last page) is that not everything that happens is what God wants to happen. After all, Jesus did have to pray for God's will to be done, it wasn't a given. That's the only way that I can approach the issue without leaving my heart and mind reeling. We don't need to scratch around in the midst of abject pain, desperately looking around for a reason. The conclusion I have come to is that despite the mess, despite things happening outside of how God would have wanted them, despite the concrete that hardens and covers our lives, God will find a way to grow flowers through the cracks if we let him. Blooming concrete. Through all things, even paving slabs, God works for the good of those who love him. Nothing can ever prevent that upward momentum of goodness and purpose. Maybe that's why I felt such a silly connection with the dandelion. It taught me an important lesson: that good can still come even if it begins in less than ideal conditions. That beauty can exist in the midst of pain and that growth can come from the darkness. Importantly for someone who struggles with church often only presenting the positive, this view of providence also allows me a grip on reality. Although the flower is beautiful, the concrete surrounding it is no less ugly or painful. It doesn't attempt to dismiss or minimize the pain. The flower just draws your eye and allows you to focus on something far more worthwhile.

To me, providence is the promise that regardless of where life takes us, nothing is beyond hope. God will always try to find a way to redeem our lives and let purpose and love break through the cracks.

* * *

I am aware that in the preceding pages, and particularly with the topic of providence, I have tackled some pretty meaty theological issues, and that each chapter has in some way come to something of a resolution or conclusion. So I want to make it clear that these questions still bother me. I have made progress, but in no way are they issues that have been ticked off my to-do list, never to be thought of again. They are not questions that I believe can be fully answered and any attempt to do so makes me feel deeply suspicious.

Under my old understanding of faith, an all or nothing approach, questions such as these presented a barrier which I couldn't cross. My ability to wrestle with them and then move on is due entirely to my new definition of faith. Faith as movement, as the willingness to keep Jesus in focus, even as everything else around me blurs. Well this is exactly that. These issues are blurry, but this way of thinking about faith allows me to plow on regardless. While still respecting and grappling with the questions, I have turned to Jesus, got as far as I could, and now I have parked them. They no longer prevent forward movement.

January 2019

It's hard not to fall into the trap of thinking that resolving all of my questions would provide an instant fix. That the fatigue, depression and anxiety would just dissolve away.

It's a surprising trap, considering that I can look at friends who are Christians and clearly see that they face similar struggles. Never have I believed that faith and mental health problems are mutually exclusive. But part of me secretly hopes that they might be for me.

The painfully honest question and significant hurdle that underpins these thoughts is this: what is the point in believing if it doesn't make any difference? And if suffering is still a very present part of it, how can it not be a disappointment? Does faith actually change anything?

Maybe not anything that can be spotted from the outside. But there is at least one part of faith that I think could have a profound aspect on my experience of life, if only I could believe it was really true. Heaven. New creation. Knowing that whatever happens, all things will be put right. Escape from the pressure of living as though this life is it and that anything that taints it ruins your one and only chance. And above all, the full stop removed from death. It would be a seismic shift in perspective. Suffering not erased, but balanced with the hope of restoration.

Anxiety not cured, but dulled by the assurance that everything actually will be okay in the end. Fatigue still draining, but overshadowed by the promise that all things, including broken bodies, will be made new.

I'm not sure why I find it so unbelievable. I observe the same promise on a small scale every year, watching the seasons come and go, new life emerging from plants that withered away months before. But sizing it all up to encapsulate the whole earth? That we can be reborn, restored, healed? It sounds too much like a fairy tale.

Look up. Look up. Look up.

Part IV

A Glimpse of Something Different

A Glimpse of Something Different

Head into heart

Picking away at bits of theology before piecing it back together again renewed my mind. It gave me confidence that Christianity could withstand my objections. It helped reassure me that it didn't have to be a choice between my fairy-tale idea of God or nothing at all. My intellect, which had spent years muttering cynical and disruptive questions under my breath, felt refreshed and engaged.

But faith cannot exist solely in your head. It has to connect with your whole being. And my doubt was never simply a question of intellectual misunderstanding. Running parallel to my cerebral renewal was something far more challenging and painful. The healing of my heart.

Rather than misunderstandings or confusion about doctrine or theology, the starting point for this quest was something much tougher to unpick and it had several strings to its bow. Firstly, those years of hanging to the coat tails of others had had a devastatingly deep impact on my understanding of what being a Christian looked like. Spending so long in a state of twisted comparison, I believed my faith would never be real unless it was identical to the faith of those around me. To phrase it more emotively, this is what I believed: that I was broken and I wouldn't be fixed until I looked like them. The truth that had slowly dawned on me was that I hadn't been searching for faith, I had been searching for a particular expression of faith. At some point, I had narrowed my options, reducing God to something unrecognizably small.

But alongside that, and underpinning it, was the sad reality that my early years of doubt had had far reaching consequences on my mental and physical health. The impact of the trauma was multilayered and probably still not completely transparent to me, but I suppose the problem boiled down to this: I was trying to connect with God, trying to muster the hope to believe that he loved me and trying to accept that my faith and experience of God was valid when I didn't even like myself. When I spent most of each day in a perpetual state of anxiety, depression, physical fatigue and mental exhaustion.

Movement in this area has been slow and it is still a work in progress. But persevering has allowed me to catch a glimpse of something different. Cracks in the concrete.

June 2019

Rotate the diamond and catch another reflection. A different view of the same whole. In my case, the possibility that all of this has been an attempt to achieve the wrong goal. It has become abundantly clear that I see myself as a problem that needs fixing. My questions, my doubts, they are wrong and need to be made right. My life cannot resume until they are, and I am drowning in the sense of urgency and pressure that that brings.

What would this search look like if I could extract myself from the twisting thorns of failure and comparison? If I could find a way to accept how I feel without seeing it as a problem? To accept that life continues and that the end goal is not necessarily to fit the mold?

Not broken, just different.

No easy feat given the impact that these years have had on my self-esteem. To have the confidence and determination to discover my own place after years of trying to fit into a seemingly impossible form requires an acceptance of self and circumstance that I don't seem to possess.

Consider this scene. Watching someone doing a jigsaw puzzle. Making headway with the sky, the sea, the hills, only to pick up a pair of scissors and snip away at a particular piece in order to make it fit. Changing its shape, cutting off corners and unique edges, just to force it to slot into the wrong puzzle. Clearly able to see a different jigsaw close by, in which the piece could have fitted into with no problem. Ridiculous, yet disturbingly familiar.

Goal posts moved then, direction changed. A move away from the pain and guilt that festers in seeing myself as the problem. An end to the attempt to find faith that conforms to the exact blueprint presented to me by my particular circle and culture.

Instead, what? I don't know. I don't know what that would look like. Not only have I lost confidence in myself, but I'm trapped on the same track, up and down, round and round, with no breathing space to consider a different route. These are also not my dominant thoughts. They quickly disperse, to be replaced by the desire to fit in with my community. To just be normal. But wouldn't it be nice? To find a way to let the steam out of the pressure cooker? To find that there has been a space waiting for me all along, one which doesn't require me to snip away at parts of myself in order to fit.

Encounter

The time had come to reassess. To consider the impact of trying so desperately to fit the mold. To try and feel at home within my own body and experience of life. Immediately obvious to me was this: I was fixated on the idea of overwhelming physical or emotional experience or miraculous intervention as the only proof of God and the only confirmation of faith. I wanted to witness writing in the sky, for a stranger to approach me in the street and tell me the innermost secrets of my heart, or to hear Jesus audibly speak to me. I wanted an in-your-face, all-singing, all-dancing encounter with God. And I was particularly focused on an emotional encounter, on faith felt as feeling. Don't misunderstand me; I don't believe that an encounter of this type is wrong. I know lots of people that have experienced God in this way (maybe not the sky writing). People who have literally seen legs grow in front of their eyes in miraculous healings. The problem was that my unhealthy compare and contrast approach to other people's faith had led to my definition of encounter narrowing only to this. It convinced me that encounters of this magnitude were the only option available.

Over the last few years, I have made a huge effort to investigate the Christian faith as thoroughly as possible. Driven of course by the hope that I would read or hear something that gave me my light bulb moment, it has also hugely expanded my biblical and theological knowledge. I have read the Bible from cover to cover, worked my way through theology textbooks and Christian books and listened to countless podcasts. I did this to try to grapple with my doubt, but also because I felt as though I had over a decade of knowledge to catch up on; that I had clocked out before I reached the point where my fledgling faith had a proper chance to grow up. I approached it as research, purely intellectual, hoping to be convinced through clever words and arguments, or maybe be so thoroughly unconvinced that it became easy to walk away. What I wasn't expecting were the passages and phrases that pinged out of the pages of the Bible, that seem to have been written just for me. Theology that blew the Bible open and showed me its depth, intricacy and richness.

It took a while to notice that I wasn't giving these moments any value. They weren't what I was looking for, or what I thought an encounter looked like, so I dismissed them. I thought I needed to be seeking adrenaline filled moments, the miraculous and sensational. Legs growing back. I presumed that it could only be a true encounter for me if it looked the same as that. I was focused completely, as society compelled me to, on the individualistic emotional experience, on knowing my thoughts through my feelings, and by holding myself up against other people. I became blinkered through comparison, unable to recognize God in the subtle, gentle whispers. I was blind to the glimpses of a different kind of encounter.

Over time, I began to identify other instances where I got the same sense of something pinging into my brain. Things that seemed to appear from nowhere, instantly grabbing my attention, things that gently but insistently tapped at my heart. Small prompts and moments of goodness and healing that diluted the pain in my cloudy heart. I will whisper this so that my cynicism can't hear: these were moments which other people might easily attribute to the Holy Spirit.

Although my threads of faith remain a vital part of this journey and are similar in their individual accumulation, these moments felt different. The main difference was their source. The threads that I have presented have all come from within me. They are mostly rational, painfully thought through and considered over long periods of time. These moments where I felt a tapping at my heart were external. Thoughts or ideas that appeared in my brain, distinct from anything else I had been concentrating on. They were not the result of the endless churning of my poor brain. And the meaning of them was not something that I had to ponder, they were instantly clear, although further levels of meaning often developed over time. They were moments of an altogether different kind. The train song, the image of a man kneeling as I offered my heart and the pinging passages were the first moments of this kind, and I will hesitantly offer some more in what follows.

Please don't misunderstand me. This isn't the moment where the tale suddenly flips and I recount an undeniable experience of God. That should be clear from the fact that these nudges haven't found a place on my embroidery hoop. I weighed them up with deep suspicion. They went totally against what I had conditioned myself to expect and what I saw as a valid encounter of God. I also had to deal with a sense of disappointment tainting the edges of these moments. I struggled to see them as equally important and meaningful as the more extravagant, high octane types of encounter. But there wasn't much point to any of this if I wasn't willing to at least pay attention and be open to a response, even if it wasn't the one that I was looking for.

Tap: absorb

Over the course of this book, I have touched on my attempt to convince myself of faith by gaining knowledge. But what I failed to admit was that this search had all the hallmarks of an addiction. My search for answers became obsessive. Desperate. Insatiable. Listening to multiple podcasts, watching online sermons, reading every book I could get my hands on. I carried on and on, never satisfied.

There is no denying that some of this research helped. It forced me to identify places where I had got the wrong idea and formed the foundation for my reconstruction of parts of Christianity. But I took it too far. I moved from one book to another without giving myself time to digest and pause. Once again, I became dependent on others and lost trust in my own opinions. My head became filled with so many people's voices that I drowned out all hope of ever finding my own.

* * *

Contrary to what many people seem to assume, the way to keep plants alive is not to water them as frequently as possible. Of course plants need water, but they are also at risk of drowning if the soil becomes too saturated. As well as water, they need air. Time and space to use the water to grow. The parallel with my intellectual waterlogging should be clear. I was at risk of not only drowning myself, but also flooding out all the other nourishment that my brain had absorbed. But rather than just being a helpful metaphor, this came as another moment where I felt a discernible jolt at my heart. I read the phrase "water well" as I have done countless times over the years, but this time, the meaning shifted.

The message seemed clear. I needed to slow down. Trust myself. Focus my limited energy on one thing at a time. Give myself a chance to let the things that I was reading settle. Let the water absorb. And discover, possibly for the first time, my own voice. It was a far cry from an overwhelming emotional experience of God's presence. But it was a moment that changed my approach, restored some confidence and calmed my mind. It was a moment where my cloudy mind was almost imperceptibly diluted.

This tap didn't put an end to my love of reading. I will always love books and I still read more than the average person (although far more fiction and far less theology). The pile of books on my night stand often threatens to collapse onto me as I sleep. But my reason for reading has changed. I no longer use other people's stories and opinions as medication to keep my faith alive. The desperation has lifted. Instead, I read out of genuine curiosity. I read in order to widen my experience and understanding. I read for joy.

Tap: drought

Since that day in the toilet cubicle, I had been haunted by the question of whether I was, or had ever been a Christian. Whether I was saved, safe or enough. It took a long time to recognize the root of that feeling: fear. The fear of dying before I believed myself to be fixed, the fear of an eternity spent in hell if I couldn't manage to convince myself that it was all true. The messages that I had received were that you got through seasons of doubt by using your maturity and strength to remember past times of faith. But as I didn't find myself able to do that, surely that meant that my faith had never been real.

* * *

When plants suffer drought, they respond by sending their roots down very deep to find water. In the long run, it makes them more robust and increases the chance that they will withstand future stress. But in my experience, it's only established plants that are able to manage this. Plants that have enough stored energy to survive while the roots dig down for nourishment. Seedlings and young plants are underdeveloped and vulnerable, they need constant food and ideal conditions to be able to grow. But what happens if the drought comes before the plants are fully established? Stop watering them and they just wither away.

Recognizing the parallel with my situation and addressing the problem from this angle, felt so forcefully as I put some frazzled seedlings onto the compost heap didn't immediately offer any hope. Most of the time, a dried out seedling was an accurate description of how I felt. But it was the difference rather the similarity that eventually gave me a bit of a nudge. I hadn't dried up and withered. Even though it didn't always feel like I had reached a source of water, no one could accuse me of not trying. The fact that I maintained the search for so long without memories of the past fueling me should mean something. There was something deep within me that refused to give up the fight.

And although the questions of security and safety still scare me sometimes, I have learnt to accept that all I can do is be honest. I'm pretty sure God wouldn't be fooled if I rocked up in heaven simply pretending to have it all worked out. Sometimes, I even summon the courage to believe that he might actually prefer me this way. That he honors and delights in my honesty. That I am enough. A person stood in her own skin, being open with herself and others and acting with integrity.

Tap: break free

Guilt has been a huge barrier to the progression of my story. It whispered persistent lies to me: it's my fault, I must have done something wrong, there must be something wrong with me. Add into that melting pot the biblical concept of having a hardened heart, and I ended up feeling very despondent. I pictured my heart as rock hard, underdeveloped, beyond all help, totally of my own doing. And in some ways, that was true. At times, I chose to harden myself, mainly through self-protection. I closed off my emotions because of the fear of what would happen if I let them out. Because I couldn't see anywhere appropriate to release them. But in other ways, it wasn't my choice. Doubt was not my fault and didn't mean that there was anything wrong with me.

Into this arena came yet another lesson from plants. The garden really is a profound place if you stop and take a look. This time it came from roses. Beautiful roses, developing in buds, waiting to open out when they are fully formed. But if the weather conspires to bring rain followed by sun, the outermost layer of the bud suffers and can end up forming a hard casing around the rest of the petals (called rose balling). The beautiful flower waiting to bloom underneath can't break through the outer shell. The only hope is that the gardener notices and very gently peels back the outer layer to let the inner flower open. And as I watched this happen, a gardener gently but lovingly releasing a beautiful rose from its ugly, hard casing, I got a tap at my heart. I felt a nudge. No overload of emotion or physical feeling. Just an almost indescribable recognition that there was something for me to take notice of. The rose had no control over the weather. In no way could it be blamed for what had happened to it. And despite appearances, the flower had been waiting underneath all along, forming and maturing despite the hard shell. It was absolutely stunning, perfect, heady with scent. If only I could see myself in that way. Release my guilt. Accept that the weather that I have endured has injured me in the same way as the rose. Accept that I too have been developing underneath all along.

* * *

For years, the connection between encounter and my self-image flowed in the wrong direction: you don't experience things like those sat next to you, therefore there must be something wrong with you. But with these taps, the tide was beginning to turn. Of course it would be possible to write them off; perhaps I was in a reflective mood, perhaps I simply had a bit of headspace which raised my awareness of my surroundings. Maybe I'm just really obsessed with plants. But I clung to them because all of the taps, without exception, spoke to my deepest insecurities. They went straight to the messiest places in my heart. The image of a man gently accepting my heart gave me worth. The train song gave me the gift of honest communication and allowed me to believe that my experience was valid. The pinging passages finally made me pay attention. Instead of believing that I needed to do and be more, "water well" told me that I was enough. Instead of letting fear dictate my head and heart, frazzled seedlings told me that I was safe. And instead of believing myself to be an unsalvageable hard shell, beyond all hope, a stunning rose told me that I was beautiful.

September 2019

It's not an optional extra, a cherry on top of an already delicious cake that would be nice but isn't necessary. There is either nothing or everything. Meaning or emptiness. I've worked myself into an uncomfortable position where I am stood on an isolated platform, with drops on either side.

I have woken up to the reality of the gap behind me. The choice of accepting a meaningless universe, an ideology that promises everything but delivers nothing of real depth. I suppose that is progress, better to see that fall for what it is, a deceptive illusion, rather than think that I can just walk away without making a decision in either direction. But I can also see the jump in front of me, the gap between where I am and where I want to be. The reality of remaining where I am, balanced precariously between the two options is that I am living as if I have already chosen emptiness.

There are three outcomes to this. Stay where I am, rooted to the spot with fear. Fall back and make the most of what I've got while I'm here. Or jump forward. Either I'll be caught or I won't. Do I not jump because I'm scared there will be nothing? Or is it because I don't understand what being caught looks like? Is a part of me postponing the decision because it delays the heartbreak of finding emptiness in front as well as behind?

The biggest barrier to making the jump forward isn't intellect or reason. Perhaps they were just distractions, something to hide behind. It all seems to stand up, it all has explanatory power. But a barrier of gut feeling remains; a combination of cynicism and fear.

The cynicism boils down to this: it is a pretty big ask. A massive shift in worldview. So much bigger and all-consuming than people seem to realize. It should deeply permeate and change every inch of us, how we see ourselves, others, our hopes, priorities, the reason and purpose of our lives, the history and future of the entire universe. An overarching reality, direction, meaning, creator, sustainer. It should be mind-blowing. How have we made it so small?

The fear is simple I suppose. I need it to be true, I'm desperate for it to be true, and I'm not sure what will happen to my already fracturing life if it isn't, or if I can never believe that it is. The combination of those two factors leads to my inaction. If it isn't all consuming, if it hasn't changed everything, then is that enough? Is that faith? I long for a light bulb moment, not a slow meandering along a path. I need it to be perfect and complete. The hole and hunger in me isn't satisfied by small whispers, moments where things seem clearer, pictures that form but can so easily be dismissed. The state I'm in means I need solidity, something tangible. Something that undeniably answers my deepest questions. Are you there, and do you love me.

Interruption

It's an almost physical feeling in my stomach. Like someone has punched me. An overwhelming cynicism. Sinking. Slipping. Drowning.

Doubt interrupts, sneaking in at any given moment. Perhaps when I am confronted with a particular phrase in a song, or the look on someone's face as they pray with such certainty and passion. Perhaps for no discernible reason at all. Just as I think I have made progress, I feel like I am back at square one. Doubts hit heavy, weighing my heart down with the pressure.

This is ridiculous. Utterly unbelievable. Too good to be true. A fairy tale. Look around you. Is this what you would expect to see if a loving God were real?

Treading their well-worn paths, doubts spiral, fester and undermine.

Look up. Look up. Look up.

Small thread of faith: life is miraculous

The assumption that science has replaced any need for God seems to be widely accepted. Although these arguments are often given in response to a form of Christianity that I don't recognize and miss the fact that the Bible doesn't actually attempt to answer the same questions as science, it is still an area that makes me feel very nervous.

It's a difficult thing to try and balance when you aren't a scientist or mathematician. I can understand the very basic arguments from both camps, but I quickly get completely out of my depth. Is it enough to know that some very committed Christians are also prominent scientists? Perhaps. But it also feels like a bit of a cop-out to a knowledge thirsty perfectionist like me.

Despite my uncertainty and confusion in this area, there is one part of scientific discovery which has pushed me further towards God. The mind-blowing statistical chances for life as we know it. Look around you. If we found life on another planet, it would be momentous. Arguably the most significant discovery in the history of the human race. Why don't we let ourselves feel such amazement at the abundant, astounding amount of life on earth?

But it's not just the emergence of life. It's also the chance that life had a planet to emerge on. The chance that the initial explosive force of the Big Bang produced gravity that was neither too strong, crushing the forming universe back in on itself, or too weak, letting matter expand out so far that no planets or complex chemistry would ever form. And that's just one of the things that needs to be exact, or fine-tuned, to allow life as we know it. If any one of these constants (like the gravitational force or electromagnetism) had a slightly different value, life wouldn't exist. And the slightly different part is extremely slight. I would try to explain the complex mathematics which demonstrates just how small the allowable difference is, but it is far beyond my level and makes my head hurt. Suffice to say, life, on earth, is miraculous.

I am by no means the first person to discover a sense of faith in this area. These arguments are often used by apologists and provide the content of books and sermon illustrations the world over. But despite it being evidence that had been presented to me countless times before from several different sources, I had to come to it in my own time. I had to approach it from the perspective of wonder, rather than being left unfazed by the dry facts and figures.

Maybe we are just lucky. Perhaps there are many other universes, or maybe ours was not the first Big Bang. We are here because we just happen to be in the right place at the right time. But that seems to take just about as much faith as accepting that there is someone or something overseeing things. This thought gives me a similar jolt to the feeling I get when I look up and picture the earth hanging there. It gives me the same shock and allows me a bit of perspective. How you get from here to belief in the Christian God or a personal relationship with him is another matter, but it is at least a step in the right direction.

Part V

Come as You Are

Acceptance

The grief I felt at my loss of certainty was so strong that in the early stages of writing my story down, I considered using the Kübler-Ross model of grief as the overarching structure. Denial, anger, bargaining, depression, acceptance. Hindsight makes it surprisingly easy to slot my story of doubt into these headings (although possibly not following such a linear order) with a particular focus on denial, bargaining and depression. I am not the first to see the similarities between the five stages of grief and the journey of lost or questioning faith. Brian McLaren discusses it in his book *Faith After Doubt*, and several close friends with a bit more objective distance pointed it out to me over the years as they saw me move from one stage to the next. Although I can see the parallel, much like my hesitancy with using the word trauma, I feel uncomfortable with using the word grief. Again, there is no comparison with those that have lost loved ones. But again, there is no escaping that my loss of faith was indeed a loss. My world shifted, forever changed.

Although it all appears to fit quite neatly now, hindsight is the key here. I don't believe that I would have been reassured by this process if someone had tried to comfort me with it on the day after the toilet moment, telling me that I would work through the stages and at some future point reach a level of acceptance. In fact, I suspect I would have been very dismissive. Not only is it tempting to believe that your experience is unique and that you won't follow the path set by others, but accepting doubt was never the plan. It wasn't that I saw acceptance as a distant, unattainable dream, it was that I didn't understand how it was possible, or how it was even a desirable goal. Frankly, the idea of never moving past doubt scared me. I craved the ideal of certainty.

Over the years, I thought that I was working hard to collect the constituent parts of faith, building towards a future point where I would be able to make a clear decision. This or that, faith or doubt, but not the two together. Just look back at the diary entry from September 2019. I tortured myself with such perfectionist, all or nothing thinking. Faith had to be perfect and complete to me to be real. I imagined myself on a high platform, with faith in front of me and doubt behind, waiting for the day when I thought I had gathered enough faith to make the jump forwards. And the accumulation did happen. Theology renewed, heart beginning to heal, threads and taps, increased maturity and self-awareness, finding community: held together, these interweaving factors reached boiling point and began to demand a response. The progress became difficult to deny. The crux was this: did I have enough to choose faith and reject doubt?

The problem I faced was that making that decision in either direction would have been a lie. There was no way to deny that I had made progress; I had a few anchor points to cling to in the darkness and my faith felt deeper and more my own than it had ever been. But there was also no denying that despite that, I still doubted. And rather than a clear distinction between the two experiences, more often than not, they were simultaneous. Not faith punctuated by moments of doubt, but the two interweaved. I was forced to consider a new alternative. That doubt and faith, for me at least, can be held together. The penny finally dropped.

It didn't have to be either/or. Perhaps the most surprising part of this realization was that it didn't feel like failure. I wasn't filled with fear. Instead, I felt peace descending. I found myself, finally, at stage five. At the dawning of acceptance. It's not something I was able to understand until I reached that point; until my lived experience presented me with no other real option. My faith was blurry. I doubted. And I wanted to follow Jesus. At that moment, and perhaps forever, they seemed to be a package deal.

Cast your mind back to the image of the gold infused cracks from earlier in the book. The idea that doubt had opened cracks which allowed faith to seep deeper. Well this is the moment that I began to see the gold. Doubt had been a destructive force in my life, one which had forced me to examine my faith, rip it apart, try life without it and finally find my way back in a new way. The cracks were still there, the doubt still present and the impact of doubt on my mental and physical health still felt, but the gold was undeniable. The accumulation couldn't be ignored. Faith and doubt. A two-sided coin. For me, acceptance is this: the willingness to stand with honesty, nothing suppressed, faith hand in hand with doubt. Accepting the presence of doubt, but also accepting and recognizing my faith. So here I am, guilt released, eyes screwed closed, arms flung high, waiting for the lifebelt. Wondering whether you really can come as you are.

From the moment in the toilet cubicle until many years later, doubt had left me paralyzed. Constantly questioning my intentions, not sure how to engage corporately or individually. Living trapped behind a mask gave me a fear of doing anything that made me feel like a hypocrite. The outcome was that I often ended up doing nothing at all. Acceptance has allowed me to write myself back into the story. It has lifted the paralysis and allowed me to get involved, to engage and to offer what I can. Let me be clear: acceptance doesn't mean that I have suddenly gained the ability to pass through life in a serene, daydream like state of happiness where nothing is able to touch me. Acceptance also doesn't mean that taking part in the narrative is free from problems. Praying and worshiping without feeling like a fraud, engaging in community without feeling ashamed and isolated, reverting to old, black and white definitions of faith: all these issues are still difficult to navigate. I am diluted, but still cloudy. There is no quick fix to this. Clinging tightly to my new definition of faith is all I have to lean on. But acceptance is accompanied by determination. One foot in front of the other I will persevere, because the truth is that walking away no longer feels like an option. I've finally accepted that as well as doubt, I have faith.

Belonging

Caught by habit and the fact that I hadn't ever known a different life, I carried on attending the same church for 5 years after I had finished working there. I tried to open up to a select few people, but it was pointless. I wasn't brave enough to be completely honest, and even if I had been, the truth of what had happened hadn't yet become clear to me so there was no way that I could communicate it to others. The actual lived experience of my story didn't progress as smoothly as the chapter by chapter narrative arc that this book implies. There were long gaps of nothingness. Simply put, I was a confused mess.

After I had left, I attended a different church. Maybe it was the guilt, maybe it was that I didn't know what else to do on a Sunday morning. Nothing was ever asked of me and I didn't offer anything in return. I never made it past polite conversation. It was the classic cliché of hoping that a change would fix things. Perhaps the grass will be greener. Maybe it's the situation, not me. Maybe the painful memories attached to that particular church are what stop me from moving forward. The time spent at the other church was silent. Looking back, it feels now as though I was sleepwalking through life. So hardened and shut down that nothing was going to break through my defenses.

A few years later, things were pretty desperate. Sundays were skipped with increasing frequency, excuses easy to come by. With the benefit of hindsight, it seems now as though this was a crucial crossroads; another point where I could have headed off into the sunset without a backwards glance. But around that time, I started to have vivid dreams about going back to my old church. I do see what you're thinking. That the dreams were a big, flashing, neon road sign from God to lead me past the crossroads and onto the "right" path. Perhaps. I was so closed off to believing that anything could be God that writing this up is honestly the first time that I've ever considered the timing and source of those dreams. My brain is a stubborn beast. This was nearly 6 years after I had left, and the intent of them was clear. I had to go back. My initial reaction was anger. I was cross with myself for entertaining any sense of nostalgia. Had I forgotten so soon how being there made me feel? Surely the shame I felt would stop me from ever crossing the threshold of the building?

The dreams continued and a few months later (in an uncharacteristically decisive move), I turned up one Sunday. Nothing spectacular happened. I don't even remember what was said or sung. But just being there, facing the ghosts, felt powerful. Healing. It felt like coming home. For the first time, I stood there with integrity. It was, of course, also extremely painful. The memories, the reminder of what I had lost and where I might have been if things hadn't gone the way they did. During the first few months of attending, I would hold back tears through every service. I had to fight the urge to leave from the moment I stepped through the doors. I didn't let anybody see. In fact, on a few occasions I did leave. I sat on a nearby bench, struggling to control my scared, shaking body. I had to imagine zipping up my whole body just to keep myself together. The only thought that kept me going was that it was probably better to feel like that in church than feel nothing at all. Being there broke through the hardened extremity.

Working out how to behave was, and still is, hard. How to come as I am. The practicalities of doubt lived in community, forming new relationships while keeping my integrity intact. I am determined not to give the wrong account of myself and end up living another lie. But it's not the kind of thing you can blurt out all in one go over coffee. I don't want to scare people off.

I'm well aware that others in my position have come to a place of acceptance with their doubt but have decided against returning to church. Especially people whose doubt is heavily linked to an experience in church. I can't pretend that I haven't considered it. Church is hard. Really hard. And there are all kinds of factors involved in making these decisions. For some people, it isn't safe. For now, my decision is to stay. There is a cost to attending, but for me, the allure of community outweighs it. The potential of a family, a body. I need people to draw me out of my own head and spur me into action. And while others might find these kinds of relationships outside the walls of a particular building, for now, I have found them within church.

Church is far from perfect. The past repeats itself in some ways. But despite everything, a small part of me feels like I belong.

* * *

Returning, I didn't even consider asking if I could join the worship team. Not only were the memories too painful, but I couldn't imagine that I would be wanted. Surely people on stage needed to have unquestionable and unquestioning faith. Comparison quickly seeped in and I wrote myself out of the story. I don't fit the mold of what I see on stage, I'm not required.

Eventually, I was asked. A one off, to fill an emergency gap. I was honest, and to my surprise, I was still wanted. I played. It felt different to any other time I had played, perhaps because I had never before played with integrity. I expected to feel embarrassed, confused and nervous. And I did feel those things, but I also felt unexpected joy; not a word I would ever use lightly. I genuinely smiled, and for a brief moment it felt as though I could feel someone else's smiles beaming at me.

I haven't played again. Although that one occasion was surprisingly positive, it showed me that my first steps walking hand in hand with faith and doubt were proving shaky. Not surprising I suppose, as it was a complete overhaul of my understanding of God, of faith and of Christianity, all playing out in the same building and with the same people where not long ago, it all meant something completely different.

Remembering the progress that I've made when I'm actually sat in the church building is hard. If I'm not careful, my physical and mental barriers automatically go up. Even though I've made the conscious choice to attend, cynicism and fear often threaten to take over. I can be prone to override the positive and expect the negative. The paths of doubt and despair have become so familiar that my mind has a hard time finding a different route. Retraining my thought patterns requires time, patience and an atmosphere of safety. My body needs to be utterly convinced that there is no threat. Physically shaking, a symptom of extreme anxiety, is a clear sign that there is still a way to go. Renewal, acceptance, healing: it's a slow process. But I will carry on. I've got the rest of my life to work out how to be a doubtful Christian, still contributing, still part of the conversation. One thing is certain: I will use my voice and my experience to let others hiding in the pews know that they are not alone. I will do my utmost to talk about doubt at every opportunity, to break the fear and increase its visibility. If God is big enough to handle our questioning, hesitations, anger and doubts, then surely church is too.

River

People come to faith in different ways. Dramatically or gradually. With an explosion, or with a slow awakening. In a world so heavily influenced by the click-bait, curated, highlight reel model presented by social media, the gradual option can often feel like failure, especially if doubt is your ever present friend. But both are valid. Both are genuine.

It is abundantly clear to me (and probably you if you've read this far) that my journey of faith belongs to the gradual category. But one of the final things to click into place in this process has been to recognize and accept that gradual doesn't necessarily mean smooth. Gradual movement to faith, to Jesus, can still look very messy.

For a long time, I had pictured my story as being a bit like a train journey. I thought it fitted well; trains take you from where you are to the place you want to end up. You have to intentionally commit to the journey, but once on board, your destination is certain. I placed myself at the train station, having at least bought a ticket, and at best trying to find my seat on the train.

Without noticing, I had fallen into the seductive trap of desiring a prescribed and ordered journey from A to B. No effort required once on board, neat lines and tick boxes rather than the twists and turns of real life. A one-time decision that sealed my fate rather than a daily choice to make the same decision again and again.

A friend patiently but firmly pointed out how ill-suited it was. An idealized fairy tale conversion and an example of trying to cram myself into the wrong jigsaw puzzle. As much as I want that kind of experience, it simply isn't the way that I move through the world. Instead, she suggested a messy, frustrating and altogether more realistic image. A rowing boat, drifting along a stream. Sometimes meandering, sometimes going off course and getting stuck in the bushes, sometimes picking up speed and going over rocks. Straining to remain in the current, but never leaving the river.

Wherever I end up, whatever challenges come, I hope that this journey has given me the courage to remain in the river. To continue to press forward. Even on the darkest days, when the only thread that I can cling to is the thought of the earth hanging in space like a marble.

Chapter one

This is not the end to the story that you might have anticipated (unless you began by flicking to the back in hope of finding out the ending, I salute you). There has been no spectacular light bulb moment, no undeniable adrenaline filled experience. The assumption is forgivable; it is not often that stories of doubt are presented before the sufferer believes that they are cured, with the doubts simply an unpleasant memory. I did promise you a story from the middle, and I wasn't lying. Accepting doubt rather than eliminating it doesn't quite fit our idea of a happy ending.

Of course that is what I had hoped for. An all-in, dramatic moment of total conversion that zapped the questions away completely. Doubt to faith, with a clear defining line between the two. That moment in the toilet cubicle pushed me overboard. Straight into the deep end with no arm bands, outside the lines and neat edges of my childhood faith. It was natural to crave certainty, to return to what I thought I had known and to what I thought faith had to look like. I had a desperate need for answers; I wanted to end up with doubts assuaged and to feel firmly settled within slightly expanded lines and slightly bigger edges. I wanted to feel like my life was following an upward graph, an ever progressing narrative that indicated that I had made more progress than it felt like and that I didn't have long left to wait before I could move from doubt to faith.

Instead, I find myself coming to an unexpected conclusion. That doubt is not failure. That its presence does not cancel out faith. And that it is possible to live in the tension between being uncertain but still feeling captivated by Jesus. Sacred confusion, water in the wilderness. Instead of certainty, I have found holy mystery. A God who seems to enjoy questions, and honors those who wrestle with him. Like Jacob, my fight has not left me untouched, and I may walk with a spiritual limp for the rest of my life, but it was only through that struggle that Jacob was touched and blessed by God. There is no denying that this tension is uncomfortable, but I truly believe that doubt and faith are not mutually exclusive.

I expected a linear path from doubt to faith. The reality is a journey which doesn't delineate as much between the two extremes.

There are still peaks and troughs to my faith and doubt, still questions and days which are particularly hard to bear. But the upward shift is that I am no longer scared. I am able to view doubt as simply doubt, rather than through the lens of shame, guilt and terror. Bad days are far less likely to trigger overwhelm or rock bottom. The threads and taps serve as a pause button. The whole thing is no longer an impenetrable cloud. I have taken a deep breath and ventured within the darkness to take a look at the component parts, and I have dissolved its cumulative power. And despite my fears, I haven't crumbled under the weight of it all.

* * *

A question that bubbles up quite often is what I would do if I had the power to change the past. The chance to avoid the conference, the tipping point, and carry on with my faith the way it was. The truth of that moment in the cubicle, charged with doubt, betrayal and disappointment is that I lost faith in the God that I believed in. What I have learned since is that I was absolutely right to. The God I believed in was a fantasy. So the answer is no. I wouldn't change the past. Doubt forced me to reconsider, tear apart my beliefs, and dig as deep as I could. As painful as this process has been, it was necessary. These long years of doubt haven't been a hoop to jump through, something to battle past and then do my best to forget. Whatever the outcome, they have shaped me, refined me, and forced me to discover far more about myself and my faith than bumbling along trying to pretend everything was fine would ever have done. Hindsight has allowed me to see small flowers starting to grow through the cracks in the concrete. Cracks which are streaked with gold.

Instead of an ending, this is the beginning of a new chapter. One where doubts are welcome. One where I can lay a claim on faith provided that I keep moving towards Jesus. Provided that my heart and head keep turning towards him like a flower following the sun.

I haven't found what I wanted to find, an answer to all my questions. Instead I have found something altogether more precious, sustainable and holy. A new way to approach faith and a new way to carry doubt.

Epilogue: Over to you

Let's talk about doubt. Not a phrase that I have ever heard in church, whether spoken from the pulpit or whispered in the pews. And I can't help but wonder how different my story might have been if it was. If experiencing doubt hadn't been inextricably linked with shame, isolation and fear. The desire to offer my story to others came as a surprise reaction to this wall of silence. Despite what you have read, I am an extremely private person. Very few people in real life know what goes on in my head. Regardless, I have shared it (thanks in part to the support and encouragement of the community I have found online) with nothing left out, simply because the loneliness I experienced in those early years of doubt is not something I will ever forget. I wrote for others facing the same, but I also wrote for the version of me that lived through this many years ago. There is something deeply psychologically healing about writing words of comfort to a younger version of yourself and becoming a safe place for others treading the same path. And that's why I chose to offer this in its raw and uncomfortable state. To do justice to the process. I haven't toned down the anger or pain or removed the inconsistencies, the opinions that chop and change. The hardest parts to share were the diary entries, particularly the ones where I went on to dramatically change my thinking or my approach (September 2019, I'm looking at you). But what's the point of any of this if I can't be honest? How would a muted and polished version be any comfort to anyone facing something similar? When it happened to me, I needed honesty. I needed to know that someone had felt the same way and thought the same things. It is a natural human trait to try and forget the darkest times once we have reached the light, but glossing over them in the retelling can leave people in similar situations feeling as though no one else understands.

Eventually, I did find the voices of others who were honest. By sharing their stories and their hard won wisdom, they slowly managed to convince me that although it felt like it at the time, my experience was not unique. My gratitude goes especially to Rachel Held Evans. I wish I had found her books years before I did. My story is my own, my experience deeply personal, but it also echoes the stories of others. Many people have occupied the same position, regardless of denomination, country and upbringing. I have learnt to recognize people who have experienced doubt in the same way as me, mainly through the language they use. Unraveled, crumbled, lost, disintegrated, undone, dissolved. We share a similar lexicon because there don't seem to be any other words that come close. Shame tells us that we are alone. That we are so broken that there is no one else that has fallen to our level. And convincing you how untrue that is gave me the drive to add my story to the others.

So, it's over to you. If you recognize yourself in my words, or you are going through something even vaguely similar, then I hope that my story has made you realize that you aren't alone. You aren't an exception or an oddity. If you need further convincing or reassurance, read some of the books listed in the further reading section. And if you have read this in order to support someone else, then I hope that my words have given you a starting point.

I'm often asked for specific suggestions of how people can

approach their doubts and I find it a very difficult question. There is no one right way to experience doubt and it follows that there is no one right way to tackle it. I'm not presenting my story as a template for anyone else to follow. One size doesn't fit all. The only advice I feel able to give is an extension of why I offer this book: try and find safe communities in which you can voice your doubts so that shame loses its grip.

To close, please allow me to repeat myself. For I know firsthand how difficult these words can be to believe.

Doubt is normal.

Doubt is not failure.

You are not alone.

Author biography

Kat Wordsworth experienced a prolonged period of crippling doubt, which inconveniently began while she was working for a church. Having discovered first hand that doubt still carries a significant stigma, she is passionate about making doubt a more accepted and less feared conversation within Christian culture. She shares her story of messy, doubtful faith on Instagram (@ about_doubt), where she is valued for her honesty, compassion and willingness to talk about things that others would prefer to ignore.

Further reading

What follows is a list of books that have helped me in my story. Some are stories of doubt and faith. Some are stories from the middle. Some are theological books which helped me to sort through my confusion. Some have nothing to do with faith but have spoken to me in other ways. In no way is this list complete and in no way does it reflect everyone's experience of life, faith and church. If you feel that something obvious is missing, feel free to contact me via Instagram (@about_doubt). I'm always delighted to add to the tower of books on my night stand.

Rob Bell, *Velvet Elvis* (Zondervan, 2005).

Sarah Bessey, *Out of Sorts* (Darton, Longman & Todd, 2015).

Kate Bowler, *Everything Happens for a Reason* (Random House, 2018).

Shane Claiborne, *The Irresistible Revolution* (Zondervan, 2006).

John Mark Comer, *The Ruthless Elimination of Hurry* (Hodder & Stoughton, 2019).

Peter Enns, *The Sin of Certainty* (HarperOne, 2016).

Jostein Gaarder, *Sophie's World* (Phoenix, 1996).

Florence Gildea, *Lessons I Have Unlearned* (Circle Books, 2021).

Pete Greig, *God on Mute* (David C Cook, 2020).

Matt Haig, *Reasons to Stay Alive* (Canongate Books Ltd, 2015), *Notes on a Nervous Planet* (Canongate Books, 2019).

Rachel Held Evans, *Faith Unraveled* (Zondervan, 2010), *Searching for Sunday* (Nelson Books, 2015), *Inspired* (Nelson Books, 2018).

Timothy Keller, *The Reason for God* (Hodder & Stoughton, 2008).

C.S. Lewis, *Mere Christianity* (Collins, 2012), *The Problem of Pain* (Collins, 2012).

Michael Lloyd, *Café Theology* (Alpha International, 2005).

Charlie Mackesy, *The Boy, the Mole, the Fox and the Horse* (Ebury

Press, 2019).

Alister E. McGrath, *Christian Theology: An Introduction, 6th Edition* (Wiley-Blackwell, 2016).

Justin McRoberts and Scott Erickson, *Prayer: Forty Days of Practice* (WaterBrook, 2019).

Rachael Newham, *Learning to Breathe* (SPCK, 2018).

Brian D. McLaren, *A New Kind of Christianity* (Hodder & Stoughton, 2011), *Faith after Doubt* (Hodder & Stoughton, 2021).

K.J. Ramsey, *This Too Shall Last* (Zondervan, 2020).

Richard Rohr, *Falling Upward* (SPCK, 2012).

Tyler Staton, *Searching for Enough* (Zondervan, 2021).

Ann Voskamp, *One Thousand Gifts* (Zondervan, 2010).

Tom Wright, *New Testament for Everyone* series (SPCK, various), *Simply Christian* (SPCK, 2006).

Philip Yancey, *A Skeptic's Guide to Faith* (Zondervan, 2003), *Prayer* (Hodder & Stoughton, 2006), *The Question That Never Goes Away* (Hodder & Stoughton, 2013), *Disappointment with God* (Zondervan, 2015).

CIRCLE
BOOKS

CHRISTIAN FAITH

Circle Books explores a wide range of disciplines within the field of Christian faith and practice. It also draws on personal testimony and new ways of finding and expressing God's presence in the world today.

If you have enjoyed this book, why not tell other readers by posting a review on your preferred book site. Recent bestsellers from Circle Books are:

I Am With You (Paperback)
John Woolley

These words of divine encouragement were given to John Woolley in his work as a hospital chaplain, and have since inspired and uplifted tens of thousands, even changed their lives.
Paperback: 978-1-90381-699-8 ebook: 978-1-78099-485-7

God Calling
A. J. Russell

365 messages of encouragement channelled from Christ to two anonymous "Listeners".
Hardcover: 978-1-905047-42-0 ebook: 978-1-78099-486-4

The Long Road to Heaven,
A Lent Course Based on the Film
Tim Heaton
This second Lent resource from the author of *The Naturalist and the Christ* explores Christian understandings of "salvation" in a five-part study based on the film *The Way*.
Paperback: 978-1-78279-274-1 ebook: 978-1-78279-273-4

Abide In My Love
More Divine Help for Today's Needs
John Woolley
The companion to *I Am With You*, *Abide In My Love* offers words of divine encouragement.
Paperback: 978-1-84694-276-1

From the Bottom of the Pond
The Forgotten Art of Experiencing God in the Depths of the Present Moment
Simon Small
From the Bottom of the Pond takes us into the depths of the present moment, to the only place where God can be found.
Paperback: 978-1-84694-066-8 ebook: 978-1-78099-207-5

God Is A Symbol Of Something True
Why You Don't Have to Choose Either a Literal Creator God or a Blind, Indifferent Universe
Jack Call
In this examination of modern spiritual dilemmas, Call offers the explanation that some of the most important elements of life are beyond our control: everything is fundamentally alright.
Paperback: 978-1-84694-244-0

The Scarlet Cord
Conversations With God's Chosen Women
Lindsay Hardin Freeman, Karen N. Canton
Voiceless wax figures no longer, twelve biblical women,
outspoken, independent, faithful, selfless risk-takers, come to life
in *The Scarlet Cord*.
Paperback: 978-1-84694-375-1

Will You Join in Our Crusade?
The Invitation of the Gospels Unlocked by the Inspiration of
Les Miserables
Steve Mann
Les Miserables' narrative is entwined with Bible study in this book
of 42 daily readings from the Gospels, perfect for Lent or anytime.
Paperback: 978-1-78279-384-7 ebook: 978-1-78279-383-0

A Quiet Mind
Uniting Body, Mind and Emotions in Christian Spirituality
Eva McIntyre
A practical guide to finding peace in the present moment that will
change your life, heal your wounds and bring you a quiet mind.
Paperback: 978-1-84694-507-6 ebook: 978-1-78099-005-7

Readers of ebooks can buy or view any of these bestsellers by
clicking on the live link in the title. Most titles are published in
paperback and as an ebook. Paperbacks are available in traditional
bookshops. Both print and ebook formats are available online.

Find more titles and sign up to our readers' newsletter at http://
www.johnhuntpublishing.com/christianity. Follow us on Facebook
at https://www.facebook.com/ChristianAlternative.